High Interest Easy Reading

A Booklist for Junior and Senior High School Students

Sixth Edition

William G. McBride, Editor,
and the Committee to Revise
High Interest—Easy Reading
of the National Council of Teachers of English

National Council of Teachers of English
1111 Kenyon Road, Urbana, Illinois 61801

NCTE Editorial Board: Richard F. Abrahamson; Celia Genishi; Richard Lloyd-Jones; Raymond J. Rodrigues; Brooke Workman; Charles Suhor, Chair, *ex officio*; Michael Spooner, *ex officio*

Staff Editor: Rona S. Smith

Cover Design: R. Maul

Interior Design: Tom Kovacs for TGK Design

NCTE Stock Number 20970-3020

© 1990 by the National Council of Teachers of English. All rights reserved. Printed in the United States of America.

It is the policy of NCTE in its journals and other publications to provide a forum for the open discussion of ideas concerning the content and the teaching of English and the language arts. Publicity accorded to any particular point of view does not imply endorsement by the Executive Committee, the Board of Directors, or the membership at large, except in announcements of policy, where such endorsement is clearly specified.

Library of Congress Cataloging-in-Publication Data

National Council of Teachers of English. Committee to Revise High Interest—Easy Reading.
    High interest—easy reading: for junior and senior high school students/ William G. McBride, editor, and the Committee to Revise High Interest—Easy Reading of the National Council of Teachers of English. —6th ed.
      p. cm.   —(NCTE bibliography series, ISSN 1051-4740)
    Includes bibliographical references and index.
    Summary: Presents an annotated bibliography of books for reluctant readers in junior high and high school, arranged in categories, and indexed by author, title, and subject.
    ISBN 0-8141-2097-0
    1. High interest–low vocabulary books—Bibliography. 2. Junior high school libraries—Book lists. 3. High school libraries—Book lists. 4. Young adult literature—Bibliography. 5. Children's literature—Bibliography. [1. High interest–low vocabulary books—Bibliography. 2. Bibliography—Best books.] I. McBride, William G. II. Title. III. Series.
Z1039.S5N4   1990
028.5′35—dc20   90-6657
                                                                                                      CIP
                                                                                                       AC

Contents

	Foreword	vii
	Note to the Reader	ix
1.	Adventure	1
2.	Animals	6
3.	Biography	10
4.	Death	19
5.	Ethnic	21
6.	Family Life	25
7.	Fantasy	35
8.	Folklore and Legends	41
9.	Friendship	42
10.	Growing Up	46
11.	Health	59
12.	Historical Fiction	61
13.	History	63
14.	How-to	67
15.	Humor	69
16.	Love and Romance	72
17.	Mystery	76
18.	Poetry	86
19.	Science	88
20.	Science Fiction	94
21.	Social Problems	98

22. Sports	104
23. Supernatural	108
24. Travel	113
Directory of Publishers	117
Author Index	121
Title Index	125
Subject Index	130
Editor	133

Foreword

The National Council of Teachers of English is proud to publish four different booklists, renewed on a regular rotation, in its bibliography series. The four are *Adventuring with Books* (pre-K through grade 6), *Your Reading* (middle school/junior high), *Books for You* (senior high), and *High Interest—Easy Reading* (junior/senior high reluctant readers). Conceived as resources for teachers and students alike, these volumes reference thousands of the most recent children's and young adults' trade books. The works listed cover a wide range of topics, from preschool ABC books to science fiction novels for high school seniors; from wordless picture books to nonfiction works on family stresses, computers, and mass media.

Each edition of an NCTE booklist is compiled by a group of teachers and librarians, under leadership appointed by the NCTE Executive Committee. Working for most of three or four years with new books submitted regularly by publishers, the committee members review, select, and annotate the hundreds of works to be listed in their new edition. The members of the committee that compiled this volume are listed on one of the first pages.

Of course, no single book is right for everyone or every purpose, so inclusion of a work in this booklist is not necessarily an endorsement from NCTE. However, it is an indication that, in the view of the professionals who make up the booklist committee, the work in question is worthy of teachers' and students' attention, perhaps for its informative, perhaps its aesthetic qualities. On the other hand, exclusion from an NCTE booklist is not necessarily a judgement on the quality of a given book or publisher. Many factors—space, time, availability of certain books, publisher participation—may influence the final shape of the list.

We hope that you will find this booklist useful and that you will collect the other booklists in the NCTE series. We feel that these volumes contribute substantially to our mission of helping to improve instruction in English and the language arts. We think you will agree.

Michael Spooner
NCTE Senior Editor for Publications

Note to the Reader

The committee has intended this book for students, although it may also be of use to teachers and media specialists/librarians. The students for whom the book may be useful are generally in grades 7-12 and generally nonreaders, although that is an indication of inclination, not ability. We believe that the primary audience for this edition, as in previous editions, is the student who *can* read—but often does not.

Entries are, therefore, written for students. We have not indicated a grade level or a sophistication level as a general rule; however, we have, in some instances, noted that a given book may contain mature subject matter. Nor have we suggested a reading level. We believe that reading levels are occasionally misleading and that interest will be the most significant factor.

We have looked for books that hold high interest for people in this age group and have been guided, to some degree, by accessibility. We have avoided books whose format suggests an elementary level; we have also avoided books whose content is too complex. While we have always looked for high-quality books, we have operated on the premise that the person who reads can always be helped in the search for better literature; the nonreader cannot. Thus, we have included some series literature and some "fast-read" books that will be of interest to less sophisticated readers.

Booklists generally provide information about what's available rather than what *must* be read. This list is no different. We believe, however, that these books are worth the time and effort to read; students who have tested them agree. The final test lies with the individual reader.

1 Adventure

1.1 Alexander, Lloyd. **The Drackenberg Adventure.** E. P. Dutton, 1988. ISBN 0-525-44389-4.

It is 1873, and seventeen-year-old Vesper Holly accepts an invitation to attend the diamond jubilee in the grand duchy of Drackenberg for her guardians, Brinnie and Mary. In Drackenberg, they meet Helvitius, an old enemy. By teaming up with the local gypsies, Holly fights Helvitius's plot to take the fortunes of Drackenberg as his own. Exciting adventures lead to an unusual climax.

1.2 Alexander, Lloyd. **The El Dorado Adventure.** E. P. Dutton, 1987. ISBN 0-525-44313-4.

Having risked her life in Illyria last year, green-eyed Vesper Holly, only seventeen, is now eager to explore her newest piece of property—a volcano in the republic of El Dorado in Central America. Amidst palm-thatched roofs, spicy food, and cantina music, Vesper struggles to protect her land from Alain de Rochefort, a villain who intends to use it in his plan to turn an Indian tribe's homeland into a swamp. In the jungle, her struggle with de Rochefort becomes a deadly game. Sequel to *The Illyrian Adventure*.

1.3 Borton de Treviño, Elizabeth. **El Güero: A True Adventure Story.** Illustrated by Leslie W. Bowman. Farrar, Straus and Giroux, 1989. ISBN 0-374-31995-2.

When an upstanding Mexican judge is exiled to uncivilized Baja California in 1876, his son Porfirio ("El Güero"), must travel through wilderness, storm, and silent Indians to find him. El Güero must then win the confidence of the commandante of the army garrison in order to save his father and the village of Ensenada from mutinous soldiers and American outlaws.

1.4 Carr, Jess. **Intruder in the Wind.** Commonwealth Press, 1987. ISBN 0-89227-076-4.

One beautiful spring day, Maria Fremont puts her baby son down on his blanket for a few minutes in the sun. While she is distracted by a phone call, a golden eagle swoops down, grabs the infant, and heads for its nest. Near the eagle's nesting place, Necco Tufferelli, a shell-shocked Vietnam veteran, has taken refuge. The noise of the rescue helicopters spurs Necco to action; the whimpering of an infant brings him a different message. While Necco fights with the rescue forces, time begins to run out for the baby.

1.5 Downing, Warwick. **Kid Curry's Last Ride.** Orchard Books, 1989. ISBN 0-531-05802-6.

Alex Penrose faces a long summer in 1935. He's twelve, and his parents have shipped him off to his grandmother in Sheridan, Wyoming, while they take an Atlantic cruise. There's nothing for Alex to do in Sheridan and no one to do it with. Then he meets an old man who claims to be Kid Curry, a member of the old Butch Cassidy gang. Kid would like one more fling, one more bank robbery, but he needs a partner—and Alex fits the bill.

1.6 Hallman, Ruth. **Search without Fear.** Dodd, Mead, 1987. ISBN 0-396-08924-0.

Dee's world has fallen apart. Gran, who took Dee in when her parents died, has just died herself, and Dee must go live with her commanding older brother David, a state trooper. In David's little mountain town, it's hard to make friends, so, to David's horror, Dee accepts a date with Will Snipes, the brother of a man David has sent to prison. Then David's worst fears about Will's need for revenge come true: Dee is kidnapped, Will plants a bomb, and Dee's chances of escape look slim.

1.7 Henken, Heidi. **Cobb's Cave.** High Noon Books, 1989. ISBN 0-87879-655-X.

Dusty finds a cave on Cobb's Hill and convinces Anne to explore it with her. When they do, they find a tunnel that takes them through the hill to the beach. There they meet a fisherman, Captain Jim, who tells them the story of Fast Jack, a pirate who may have buried treasure in the tunnel. Dusty decides that she will find the treasure. Later, Cobbie, a mysterious, pipe-smoking woman, clears up the mystery of Fast Jack's treasure, but the mystery of Cobbie still remains.

1.8 Paulsen, Gary. **Hatchet.** Bradbury Press, 1987. ISBN 0-02-770130-1.

Thirteen-year-old Brian Robeson is on his way to spend the summer with his father in the Canadian wilderness. Brian's parents have recently divorced, and the court has determined that Brian will spend the school year with his mother and the summer with his father. As Brian is flying to his father's engineering camp, the pilot suffers a fatal heart attack, and the plane crashes. Brian is not badly hurt, but with only a hatchet his mother has given him, will he be able to survive?

1.9 Paulsen, Gary. **The Island.** Orchard Books, 1988. ISBN 0-531-05749-6.

Fifteen-year-old Wil Neuton was not excited about having to move from the life he had just established in Madison, Wisconsin, to a small house way out in the boonies. However, that was before he discovered the island—or it discovered him—he is not quite sure which way it happened. The hours that he spends there grow into days that are filled with keen observation, studying, and learning about the life and truth of the island and about himself.

1.10 Petersen, P. J. **How Can You Hijack a Cave?** Delacorte Press, 1988. ISBN 0-440-50063-X.

Curt Carver has met his match. Lori is almost as tall as he is and can almost beat him at one-on-one, but the worst part is that she's his boss! It takes a couple of weeks, but Curt is finally settling into his job as a guide at Cathedral Caverns. Then terrorists strike, kidnapping rich Pauline and holding her hostage in the caves. Can Curt and Lori rescue her through a secret entrance? Curt discovers the courage and ingenuity needed to match Lori in this suspenseful story.

1.11 Regan, Dian Curtis. **Game of Survival.** Avon/Flare Books, 1989. ISBN 0-380-75585-8.

Nicky Brooks has big plans for Mitchell High's weekender at Camp Chautauqua in the Colorado Rockies, but those plans abruptly change on a scavenger hunt the first morning out. Nicky and a new student, Martinella Lee Prigmore, get lost when a surprise snowstorm comes in. They are joined by Nicky's archenemy, Sidney "Scruggs" Scruggman, who has been badly injured. The three are then forced to use all of their knowledge to survive.

1.12 Ruckman, Ivy. **No Way Out.** Harper Keypoint Books, 1988. ISBN 0-690-04669-3.

Danger and fear stalk six young hikers in the Zion Narrows in Utah when a flash flood turns their perfect weekend into a nightmare. Amy and Rick fight for their lives and their future together as they learn more than they may have wanted to know about each other.

1.13 Service, Pamela F. **The Reluctant God.** Atheneum, 1988. ISBN 0-689-31404-3.

Fourteen-year-old Lorna Padgett, only daughter of an archaeologist working in Egypt, loves everything Egyptian. Ameni, son of the ancient pharaoh Senusert II, wants to travel and have adventures, rather than train as a priest of Osiris. Incredibly, Lorna's love of Egypt brings her together with Ameni when she revives him from the state of suspended animation he had been in since ancient times. Forming a friendship that bridges four thousand years, Ameni and Lorna travel to England, where they find themselves in an adventure that is more dangerous than either of them ever bargained for.

1.14 Tolan, Stephanie S. **The Great Skinner Homestead.** Four Winds Press, 1988. ISBN 0-02-789362-6.

When their motor home breaks down in the Adirondack Mountains, Jenny Skinner's father decides that their family of six will become pioneers. They'll homestead there, with no electricity, no cars, and no boys for fifteen-year-old Jenny to date. As the Skinner family braves nature, some of them long for the comforts of the city, while Jenny considers overcoming her fear of snakes for a handsome college student doing rattlesnake research. All of them, though, learn about surviving, and Jenny and her sister Sarah find themselves the only people who can save their father's life. Second book in a series about the Skinner family.

1.15 Townsend, John Rowe. **The Fortunate Isles.** J. B. Lippincott, 1989. ISBN 0-397-32365-4.

The king of the Fortunate Isles has declared war, and all the healthy men of Eleni's village must join the army and fight. Hardly anyone is left behind to take care of the women and children, who are in the midst of a famine. But Eleni might be the key to an ancient prophecy. She begins a journey to the Holy Mountain of Ayos, where she hopes to find salvation for her people.

Adventure 5

1.16 Wallace, Bill. **Red Dog.** Holiday House, 1987. ISBN 0-8234-0650-4.

In the 1860s, Adam's stepfather moves his family into the Wyoming mountains. When he then leaves for Cheyenne, twelve-year-old Adam and his dog Ruff are left alone to protect Adam's mother and sister from a group of greedy prospectors. In bone-chilling action, Adam and Ruff give their family everything they have.

2 Animals

2.1 Caras, Roger A. **Animals in Their Places: Tales from the Natural World.** Sierra Club Books, 1987. ISBN 0-87156-707-5.

Meet the giant Kodiak bear as she moves her 700-pound body about Kodiak Island in search of food. Soar above cliffs with one of the few remaining California condors, and swim upstream with a salmon bent on returning to her birthplace. The author takes you into the wild and shines a spotlight on everything from pythons and elephants to panthers and wolves as they go about their daily lives.

2.2 Diggs, Lucy. **Moon in the Water.** Atheneum, 1988. ISBN 0-689-31337-3.

JoBob knows he's a misfit, he's small for a fourteen year old, and, unlike the families of the other kids at the stable where he works, his family struggles to make ends meet. Blue, the pinto at the stables, is a misfit, too. Others think Blue is only good enough to use as a teaching horse, but JoBob has been secretly training Blue to jump. His work with Blue gives JoBob both the greatest joy and the greatest sorrow that he's ever known.

2.3 Herberman, Ethan. **The City Kid's Field Guide.** Simon and Schuster Books for Young Readers, 1989. ISBN 0-671-67749-7.

Abundant wildlife is not limited to forests, rivers, marshes, and land far from civilization. For the keen observer, "wildlife" may be found in homes, backyards, parks, and the vacant lots of large cities. Illustrations and interesting facts about wildlife, dangerous and harmless, are presented in this "guide to the urban nature trail." Index included. A *Nova* book.

2.4 Hopkins, Lila. **Eating Crow.** Franklin Watts, 1988. ISBN 0-531-10499-0.

On his first day at a new school, Ezekiel Silverstein gives all of the other students the silent treatment. One of the other students, Croaker Douglas, resents this so much that he takes matters into

Animals

his own hands and attacks Ezekiel. When their teacher makes Croaker go to Ezekiel's house to apologize, Croaker finds a couple of big surprises, including Piccolo, a talking crow.

2.5 Jurmain, Suzanne. **Once upon a Horse: A History of Horses—and How They Shaped Our History.** Lothrop, Lee and Shepard Books, 1989. ISBN 0-688-05550-8.

Whether as servant, traveler, messenger, game player, racer, or friend, the horse has been the most pampered domestic animal in history—and with good reason. The horse is "the only four-legged animal that has ever changed the way humans lived, fought, worked, and played." The horse is found in folklore, legend, religion, and every form of art the world over. Index included.

2.6 Mauser, Pat Rhoads. **Love Is for the Dogs.** Avon/Flare Books, 1989. ISBN 0-380-75723-0.

Janna loves animals and works as a volunteer in a veterinarian's office. She hates her new neighbor, Bramwell Hamilton, on sight because he leaves his dog Pepper outside even when it rains. In an effort to help Pepper, Janna becomes friendly with Bramwell, and she soon learns some very interesting things.

2.7 Patent, Dorothy Hinshaw. **Where the Wild Horses Roam.** Photographs by William Muñoz. Clarion Books, 1989. ISBN 0-89919-507-5.

Horses died out on the American continent nearly 8,000 years ago, and it wasn't until the fifteenth century that the Spanish explorers reintroduced them. Today, wild horses are found in ten western states. In 1971, the Wild Horse and Burro Act was passed to protect horses and burros, and between 1971 and 1980, the wild herds grew from an estimated 17,000 to 64,000. Includes an index and a list of organizations dedicated to protecting wild horses.

2.8 Sattler, Helen Roney. **The Book of Eagles.** Illustrated by Jean Day Zallinger. Lothrop, Lee and Shepard Books, 1989. ISBN 0-688-07022-1.

Eagles are difficult to study in the wild because they are very swift and because they fly so high. However, scientists do agree that there are at least sixty species around the world and that only two of those species are found in the United States. Despite their power as hunters, their size, and their strength, these "lords of the skies" are threatened with extinction.

2.9 Saville, Lynn. **Horses in the Circus Ring.** E. P. Dutton, 1989. ISBN 0-525-44417-3.

This book takes an important part of every circus—the horses—and gives them the center ring in a show of their own. Packed with colorful pictures, it explains how the horses are trained for such things as precision teamwork, carrying a human pyramid, and stunt riding.

2.10 Shachtman, Tom. **Wavebender: A Story of Daniel au Fond.** Illustrated by Jamichael Henterly. Henry Holt, 1989. ISBN 0-8050-0840-3.

Sea-lion beachmaster Daniel au Fond sets out on a quest to find Pacifica, a cove in an ancient sea-lion legend where sea creatures and humans once lived in harmony. To find this secret place, Daniel and his tribe roam the oceans seeking a wavebender and collecting unusual allies from different species of sea creatures. After several dangerous encounters with pollution and commercial overhunting, Daniel realizes that heroic action is necessary to preserve all sea life.

2.11 Silver, Donald M. **The Animal World.** Illustrated by Patricia J. Wynne. Random House, 1987. ISBN 0-394-86650-3.

From the tiny, one-celled protozoa to the 150-ton blue whale, the animal kingdom is filled with many unique creatures. Their ways of living, playing, gathering food, mating, defending themselves, and nurturing their young are as varied as the animals themselves. Over a thousand color illustrations of animals in their natural habitats give you a glimpse of how they have evolved and how they survive. Index included.

2.12 Springer, Nancy. **Not on a White Horse.** Atheneum, 1988. ISBN 0-689-31366-7.

Twelve-year-old Rhiannon DiAngelo has always loved horses, so when she sees the ad in the newspaper about the lost white Arabian, she hops on her bike and heads out to look for it. She spots the horse several times and develops a relationship with its owner, Chickie Miller, who begins to teach her about horses. This new outlet gives Rhiannon a focus for her life and helps her to deal with her father's alcoholism and abuse.

2.13 Wallace, Bill. **Snot Stew.** Illustrated by Lisa McCue. Holiday House, 1989. ISBN 0-8234-0745-4.

"Don't play with your food," Mama always said. "Unless it's a mouse. Then it's okay." Kikki remembers her mother well, but Kikki and her brother Toby are alone. Abandoned by their mother and the other kittens, Kikki and Toby learn to live in the world of "people things." Everything is wonderful until the children that Kikki and Toby live with invent a game called Snot Stew.

2.14   Wilson, A. N. **Stray.** Orchard Books, 1989. ISBN 0-531-05840-9.

Old Father Pufftail may be getting on in years, but he's still a proud old alley cat who is pleased to share his experiences with his grandson, Kitchener. Pufftail began life innocently enough but soon discovered that not all humans are good people nor can they all be trusted. He discovered that cats, too, are imperfect, and he tries to tell his grandson that life, though not always pleasant, is generally worthwhile.

3 Biography

3.1 Aaseng, Nathan. **The Fortunate Fortunes.** Lerner, 1989. ISBN 0-8225-0678-5.

Who would have thought a train ride sixty years ago would lead to the development of the popular biscuit mix, Bisquick? Or that in order to insult a resort guest who had made him angry, a chef would slice potatoes paper thin and fry them, thus producing the first potato chips? Similar stories about other products and businesses and the people who introduced them illustrate that not only does the creation of new products take hard work and ingenuity, but the success of these products also depends upon luck. Index included.

3.2 Aaseng, Nathan. **The Problem Solvers.** Lerner, 1989. ISBN 0-8225-0675-0.

Is good help hard to find? Are you tired of straining vegetables to make baby food? Are you losing your hair and becoming bald before the age of thirty? Individuals who found creative solutions to these problems formed successful companies—Kitchen-Aid, Gerber, and Breck. These stories and others illustrate how familiar products were developed in response to a need. Index included.

3.3 Aaseng, Nathan. **The Unsung Heroes.** Lerner, 1989. ISBN 0-8225-0676-9.

If the names Earl Dickson, John Pemberton, James Spangler, Jerry Siegel, Joe Shuster, and Maria Innocentia were mentioned, would you know who they are? These people invented or helped create well-known products or businesses, but they often received little recognition—and sometimes little profit—for their ideas. However, if Band-Aid, Coca-Cola, Hoover vacuum cleaners, Superman, and Hummel figurines were substituted for the names above, you would know the products these people are associated with. Index included.

3.4 Barnes, Jeremy. **Samuel Goldwyn: Movie Mogul.** Silver Burdett Press, 1989. ISBN 0-382-09586-3.

Samuel Goldwyn was a Jewish immigrant from a Warsaw ghetto who had little money and very little schooling and who didn't even speak English. Since his only talent seemed to be selling gloves, he appeared to be an unlikely person to produce some of Hollywood's finest films. However, entirely by his own effort, he earned fame and wealth and developed a reputation for paying people very well and insisting on the highest quality. Part of The American Dream series. Index included.

3.5 Black, Sheila. **Sitting Bull and the Battle of the Little Bighorn.** Illustrated by Ed Lee. Silver Burdett Press, 1989. ISBN 0-382-09572-3.

In 1876, thousands of Sioux warriors led by Chief Sitting Bull massacred a troop of United States soldiers led by General George Custer. Custer attacked the Indians, but Sitting Bull and his people were blamed. Who was Sitting Bull, and why did he gather his people for war? Part of Alvin Josephy's Biography Series of American Indians.

3.6 Bowman, John. **Andrew Carnegie: Steel Tycoon.** Silver Burdett Press, 1989. ISBN 0-382-09582-0.

The son of Scottish weavers, Andrew Carnegie came to America at an opportune time and settled with his family in Pittsburgh. By chance the young Andrew became involved with the telegraph and, later, railroads. This led naturally to an interest in iron and steel, which made him the richest man in the world in his time. Carnegie believed that a rich person who died with a fortune intact died disgraced, so he gave most of his money away to charity, mainly to libraries, concert halls, and educational institutions. Carnegie was extremely interested in projects that would result in the improvement of society. Part of The American Dream series.

3.7 Buranelli, Vincent. **Thomas Alva Edison.** Silver Burdett Press, 1989. ISBN 0-382-09522-7.

Because he was a poor student, Thomas Edison was taken out of school at the age of seven and taught at home by his mother, who had been a teacher before marriage. Edison's father taught him the value of hard work. Later, when Edison was called a genius, he often replied with his most famous saying: "Genius is 1 percent inspiration and 99 percent perspiration." During Edison's lifetime, and because of his inventions, the world changed from gaslights and still photographs to a "world transformed by electric lights, motion pictures, and the phonograph." Part of the Pioneers in Change series. Index included.

3.8 Castiglia, Julie. **Margaret Mead.** Silver Burdett Press, 1989. ISBN 0-382-09525-1.

Born in 1901, anthropologist Margaret Mead was considered a woman ahead of her time. Even getting a college degree in the early part of this century was unusual for a girl. At an early age, she was encouraged by her grandmother to observe human relationships and actions and to make a record of those observations. Energetic, dedicated, and enthusiastic, Margaret Mead traveled all over the world and wrote many books and magazine articles about her observations. Part of the Pioneers in Change series.

3.9 Cwiklik, Robert. **King Philip and the War with the Colonists.** Illustrated by Robert L. Smith. Silver Burdett Press, 1989. ISBN 0-382-09573-1.

When the Pilgrims landed at Plymouth Rock, they entered the land of the friendly Chief Massasoit, whose name was later adopted by the state of Massachusetts. This book tells the story of Chief Massasoit's son, who saw that his father's friendliness toward the Pilgrims led only to loss of lands and death for his people. The colonists called him King Philip, and he fought his own war of independence against the newcomers. Part of Alvin Josephy's Biography Series of American Indians.

3.10 Cwiklik, Robert. **Sequoyah and the Cherokee Alphabet.** Illustrated by T. Lewis. Silver Burdett Press, 1989. ISBN 0-382-09570-7.

When the first settlers pushed westward from the eastern seaboard, they ran into a large and strong Indian tribe, the Cherokees. The Europeans wanted to force the tribe to either give up their Indian ways and accept white culture or leave their land and move away. But Sequoyah gave his people a way to hold onto their culture even while living among more and more whites. Part of Alvin Josephy's Biography Series of American Indians.

3.11 Faber, Doris, and Harold Faber. **Great Lives: American Government.** Charles Scribner's Sons, 1988. ISBN 0-684-18521-0.

You've heard the textbook explanations about America's great leaders. Now experience the stories that the leaders themselves lived. From the founding fathers to our own times, this book lets you understand the famous, the not-so-famous, and the always-important lives of those who have led our country. Index included.

3.12 Fradin, Dennis Brindell. **Remarkable Children: Twenty Who Made History.** Little, Brown, 1987. ISBN 0-316-29126-9.

Did you know that Muhammad Ali boxed on television at the age of thirteen? That Louis Braille invented the Braille system of reading at the age of fifteen? That at thirteen Anne Frank wrote her famous diary depicting life during World War II? In this book, you'll learn the amazing true stories of these and many other amazing people who achieved great tasks before the age of seventeen, including Tracy Austin, Bobby Fischer, Wolfgang Amadeus Mozart, Pablo Picasso, and Helen Keller.

3.13 Freedman, Russell. **Indian Chiefs.** Holiday House, 1987. ISBN 0-8234-0625-3.

As the pioneers of the mid-1800s moved westward, their meetings with the Native Americans were not always peaceful. Red Cloud of the Oglala Sioux, Joseph of the Nez Percé, and Sitting Bull of the Hunkpapa Sioux are three of six Indian chiefs described in this book, chiefs who led their people in times of crisis. Their stories are ones of leadership, banishment to reservations, bloodshed, unkept treaties, and bravery.

3.14 Freedman, Russell. **Lincoln: A Photobiography.** Clarion Books, 1987. ISBN 0-89919-380-3.

Using carefully chosen photographs and prints, this biography illustrates the life of perhaps our most popular president. The vivid text of the biography traces Lincoln's life, focusing on the critical period during the Civil War.

3.15 Gillies, John. **Señor Alcalde: A Biography of Henry Cisneros.** Dillon Press, 1988. ISBN 0-87518-374-3.

Texas is the home of the Alamo. It is also the home of Henry Cisneros, San Antonio's mayor. This interesting biography, complete with photographs, highlights the life of Cisneros, the first person of Mexican descent to be elected as mayor of a major U.S. city. The book includes a chapter in which the mayor offers advice to young people who want to make the most of their education and future careers. Part of the People in Focus series.

3.16 Glassman, Bruce S. **J. Paul Getty: Oil Billionaire.** Silver Burdett Press, 1989. ISBN 0-382-09584-7.

What kind of person can build one of the largest business empires in the world and still be accused of physical cowardice? J. Paul Getty was that kind of person—a man with two faces. Why would such a rich and powerful man feel the need to lie about his ancestors? Why would he say he loved his son Timmy best of all his sons and yet remain in Europe while that son was dying in Los Angeles? These questions and others make J. Paul Getty a very puzzling personality. Part of The American Dream series. Index included.

3.17 Hamilton, Virginia. **Anthony Burns: The Defeat and Triumph of a Fugitive Slave.** Alfred A. Knopf, 1988. ISBN 0-394-88185-0.

Anthony Burns, age twenty, was born a slave in Virginia and escaped to Boston in 1854. For a while he lived and worked as a free man; but one day, his former owner appeared and invoked the Fugitive Slave Act, which allowed him to take Anthony back to Virginia. The ensuing battle between the slave owners and those who fought for the rights of fugitive slaves caused riots and made necessary the calling in of federal troops. And at the center of the struggle was Anthony Burns himself, the last fugitive slave to be seized on Massachusetts soil.

3.18 Ireland, Karin. **Albert Einstein.** Silver Burdett Press, 1989. ISBN 0-382-09523-5.

Albert Einstein was gentle and sensitive and believed in peace between nations, and yet he spoke in favor of developing the atom bomb. Considered by many people to be the greatest scientist in the world, he did not talk until he was three, and some of his teachers thought he was retarded. While he hated strict discipline at school, he imposed the strictest discipline upon himself while he studied. Indeed, Albert Einstein was a man of opposites. Part of the Pioneers in Change series. Index included.

3.19 Johnson, Neil. **All in a Day's Work: Twelve Americans Talk about Their Jobs.** Joy Street Books, 1989. ISBN 0-316-46957-2.

Unique people expressing their hopes, frustrations, and rewards in word and image make the world of work truly understandable.

Twelve men and women from different ethnic groups and backgrounds share more than the typical "career" information. They describe what they like and what they don't like about their jobs, why they stay with them, and how they feel about their jobs when they go home.

3.20 Lomask, Milton. **Great Lives: Exploration.** Charles Scribner's Sons, 1988. ISBN 0-684-18511-3.

The history books say what explorers have done, but they don't always tell why they have done it or how they have felt. Go along with twenty-five of the world's greatest explorers as they trek to the poles, sail around the world, and hack their way through jungles in search of treasure.

3.21 McClard, Megan, and George Ypsilantis. **Hiawatha and the Iroquois League.** Illustrated by Frank Riccio. Silver Burdett Press, 1989. ISBN 0-382-09568-5.

The Iroquois leader Hiawatha grew up in the area that later became New York. Before the Europeans arrived, he envisioned and created an Indian government based on democracy and cooperation among tribes. Later, Ben Franklin and other white colonists learned from the Iroquois League when they were forming the United States.

3.22 Neimark, Anne E. **Ché! Latin America's Legendary Guerilla Leader.** J. B. Lippincott, 1989. ISBN 0-397-32308-5.

Ché Guevara rose from an asthmatic boyhood to become a popular leader of the revolution in Latin America. In this fictionalized biography, Neimark tells of Ché's treks through Latin America to his rise to international fame as Fidel Castro's close ally in Cuba to his defeat in Bolivia. Working until his death to free the oppressed, Ché Guevara became a hero to revolutionaries around the world. The author points out that this fictionalized account of Ché is faithful to the historical man.

3.23 Nesnick, Victoria Gilvary. **Princess Diana: A Book of Questions and Answers.** M. Evans, 1988. ISBN 0-87131-558-0.

You've heard of fairy-tale queens, but what is it like to be a true princess? Diana, Princess of Wales, shows us. Who was Diana before joining the royal family? How did she meet Prince Charles? What was their wedding like? What is her life like now? Being a princess means so much more than fancy clothing, but the clothing does help!

3.24 Pelta, Kathy. **Alexander Graham Bell.** Silver Burdett Press, 1989. ISBN 0-382-09529-4.

Alexander Graham Bell was born in Scotland and did not become a U.S. citizen until 1882. His interest in sound and speech came naturally because his father and grandfather were speech teachers, and he followed in their footsteps. As he worked with deaf students, he became more and more interested in the possibility of sending speech over an electrified wire, and in 1875, he invented the telephone. Part of the Pioneers of Change series. Index included.

3.25 Ramusi, Molapatene Collins, and Ruth S. Turner. **Soweto, My Love.** Henry Holt, 1989. ISBN 0-8050-0263-4.

A long-time associate of Nelson Mandela, Mafa Molapatene Kotoleleele Ramusi was one of the early members of the Pan Africanist Congress. In this book, Ramusi tells his own story—from his birth in a South African village to his eight-year exile in the United States because of his participation in anti-apartheid activities.

3.26 Shorto, Russell. **Geronimo and the Struggle for Apache Freedom.** Illustrated by L. L. Cundiff. Silver Burdett Press, 1989. ISBN 0-382-09571-5.

When American paratroopers jump out of airplanes today, they shout, "Geronimo!" Leader of the Apache Indians in the late 1800s, Geronimo's very name now stands for freedom fighting. But the nation Geronimo defended was his own Apache nation, and he fought troops from the United States. Why did he fight, and why did he earn such respect? Part of Alvin Josephy's Biography Series of American Indians.

3.27 Shorto, Russell. **Tecumseh and the Dream of an American Indian Nation.** Illustrated by Tim Sisco. Silver Burdett Press, 1989. ISBN 0-382-09569-3.

In what would become the state of Indiana, Tecumseh, the crouching panther, became chief of the Shawnee tribe and worked toward his dream of creating an Indian nation. When the American Colonies began the Revolution, Tecumseh chose to join forces with the British because they promised the Indians a country

Biography

of their own. In battle after battle, he proved himself brave and wise. Part of Alvin Josephy's Biography Series of American Indians.

3.28 Sufrin, Mark. **Payton.** Charles Scribner's Sons, 1988. ISBN 0-684-18940-2.

Walter Payton was an exceptional athlete, always driven to excel. The author traces Payton's life from his childhood in Mississippi to his final game as a professional football player for the Chicago Bears. Photographs and tables help illustrate Payton's many achievements as one of the best runners ever to play football.

3.29 Sullivan, George. **Great Lives: Sports.** Charles Scribner's Sons, 1988. ISBN 0-684-18510-5.

Think of the great events in sports history, and think of the people who made them happen: Babe Ruth, Muhammad Ali, Gordie Howe, Julius Erving, and many more. See the stories behind the people, and understand how the championship moments came to life.

3.30 Sullivan, George. **Mikhail Gorbachev.** Julian Messner, 1988. ISBN 0-671-63263-9.

Mikhail Gorbachev became the General Secretary of the Soviet Union on March 11, 1985. This book traces his amazing rise to power and provides an enlightening look at what's currently happening inside the U.S.S.R., including *glasnost*, the Chernobyl disaster, and recent summit meetings.

3.31 Tompert, Ann. **The Greatest Showman on Earth: A Biography of P. T. Barnum.** Dillon Press, 1987. ISBN 0-87518-370-0.

Phineas Taylor Barnum, born on July 5, 1810, is best known for his circus; however, in his life he had many other successful and not-so-successful business ventures. In his eighty-one years, he ran a general store and a newspaper, sold Bibles, operated a museum, and became famous for his love of a good joke and for his advertising feats. He also discovered General Tom Thumb and Jumbo the Elephant. This book is full of funny stories about the famous P. T. Barnum. Part of the People in Focus series.

3.32 Weidhorn, Manfred. **Robert E. Lee.** Atheneum, 1988. ISBN 0-689-31340-3.

In April 1861, Robert E. Lee turned down Abraham Lincoln's offer to command the Union Army and decided to fight for the South. He was "the best soldier in America," the man who altered the balance of the Civil War. Robert E. Lee's leadership and military brilliance kept the South alive against insurmountable odds.

4 Death

4.1 Carter, Alden R. **Sheila's Dying.** G. P. Putnam's Sons, 1987. ISBN 0-399-21405-4.

Jerry Kinkaid doesn't care that he and Sheila are an unlikely couple. She's cute and sexy, and he has fun dating her. Then, on New Year's Eve, their world turns upside down when they discover that Sheila has cancer. Only Bonnie, the Tiger Shark whom Jerry has often fought with, is willing to support him while he watches Sheila die and while he learns some very valuable lessons about living.

4.2 Ferris, Jean. **Invincible Summer.** Avon/Flare Books, 1987. ISBN 0-374-33642-3.

Robin Gregory and Rick Winn meet in the hospital when she goes in for tests and he for chemotherapy. When Robin discovers that she, too, has leukemia, she relies on Rick's antics and his thoughtfulness to help her through the bad times. Initially drawn together by a shared illness, they discover a much deeper relationship. Together they find the courage to live for the present and to face the future unafraid.

4.3 Grant, Cynthia D. **Phoenix Rising; or, How to Survive Your Life.** Macmillan, 1989. ISBN 0-689-31458-2.

Jessie can't cope with her sister Helen's death from cancer or with the tension and chaos of her family life. She panics and withdraws into a frightening dream world—until she discovers Helen's diary. Helen's words help Jessie to live, grow up, and learn to love herself and her family again.

4.4 Irwin, Hadley. **So Long at the Fair.** Margaret K. McElderry Books, 1988. ISBN 0-689-50454-3.

Ashley—talented, spirited, and beautiful—is dead. Joel, who at eighteen, has never really thought about life without her, feels betrayed by her suicide. To try to forget Ashley and to lessen his own pain, Joel goes to the state fair, giving up his identity as Joel Logan III to become Joe the dishwasher, Joe the drifter.

4.5 Mazer, Norma Fox, and Harry Mazer. **Heartbeat.** Bantam Books, 1989. ISBN 0-553-05808-8.

After Tod fixes up his shy friend Amos with the beautiful (and crack auto mechanic) Hilary, Tod and Hilary fall passionately, but secretly, in love. Then, when Amos falls desperately ill, they agree to separate in order to comfort him. After Amos's death, Tod and Hilary discover they have matured independently.

4.6 Schwandt, Stephen. **Holding Steady.** Henry Holt, 1988. ISBN 0-8050-0575-7.

After seventeen-year-old Brendon Turner's father is killed in a single-car accident on an icy road, he doesn't know how to cope with the loss. He feels angry, guilty, and sad all at once. Then his mother rents a cottage in Wisconsin for their summer vacation, and Brendon meets Courtney, who is dealing with losses of her own. Together they learn about life, acceptance, and love—and a lot about themselves.

4.7 Zindel, Paul. **A Begonia for Miss Applebaum.** Harper and Row, 1989. ISBN 0-06-026877-8.

Henry and Zelda are shocked to learn that their favorite teacher, Miss Applebaum, has retired because she is terminally ill with cancer. After visiting Miss Applebaum and bringing her a begonia plant, they are drawn into a close and stimulating relationship with her during her last days. Even though they want to help, Henry and Zelda have to come to terms with Miss Applebaum's death and with her final wish.

5 Ethnic

5.1 Cohen, Barbara. **People Like Us.** Bantam Books, 1987. ISBN 0-553-05441-4.

When Dinah Adler is asked out by the most wonderful guy at her high school, star quarterback Geoff Ruggles, Dinah's parents ask her not to go on the date. They say, "People like us shouldn't consider dating anyone who isn't the same religion." She tries to explain the situation to Geoff, but he can't help her because he doesn't understand. Will Dinah have to choose between her parents and Geoff?

5.2 Filichia, Peter. **What's in a Name?** Avon/Flare Books, 1988. ISBN 0-380-75536-X.

What do you picture when you hear the name Rose Sczylanska? Right. That's what Rose thinks, too. She's cute and has great hair and a good figure, yet she's haunted by store clerks, teachers, and potential boyfriends who can't pronounce or spell her name. Of course, she gets no sympathy from her hockey-playing brother, who thinks the name fits his image perfectly. So Rose decides to change her name. She feels great, more confident, more popular, especially with the New York University students she meets. But how does she break the news to her family? The struggle to grow up just got a new battle. Is Rose up to the challenge?

5.3 Glover, Vivian. **The First Fig Tree.** St. Martin's Press, 1987. ISBN 0-312-01762-6.

Ellen's friends and neighbors are caught up in the excitement of Roosevelt's declaration of war on Japan. But Ellen, born into slavery, doesn't seem to notice. Instead, she faces her daughter and son-in-law, who say that she must leave her home and move in with them. It will be peaceful, they tell her, and they have a granddaughter who will be company for her. The child and her great-grandmother, one too young and one too old for the war around them, must fight their battles on the home front.

5.4 Gordon, Sheila. **Waiting for the Rain: A Novel of South Africa.** Orchard Books, 1987. ISBN 0-531-05726-7.

As children, Tengo and Frikkie, one black, one white, are playmates and friends. Frikkie spends his vacations on his uncle's farm on the South African veld and dreams of the day that he will be finished with school and able to come live on the farm forever. Tengo, on the other hand, dreams of an education that will provide an escape from servitude. As they grow older, the two boys and their dreams are torn and twisted by the social system of South Africa.

5.5 Lasky, Kathryn. **The Bone Wars.** Morrow Junior Books, 1988. ISBN 0-688-07433-2.

Thaddeus Longworth is an orphaned fourteen year old in 1874 when he signs on as scout for a Harvard paleontologist, one of many who are looking for dinosaur bones. Thad does not approve of the fierce competition among the paleontologists, nor is he happy with the situation developing between the Plains Indians and the U.S. government. Thad and his English friend, Julian, decide to join forces in order to achieve their goals concerning the discovery and display of the enormous creatures who once roamed the earth.

5.6 Levitin, Sonia. **Silver Days.** Atheneum, 1989. ISBN 0-689-31563-5.

The Platt family is finally together again in America. After they escaped from Nazi Germany, Papa came to America to establish a foothold while his family stayed in Switzerland. Now they face the rigors of a new environment, a new language, and a different perspective. Lisa's ideas of what life in America will be like turn out to be quite different from the reality she finds here, but she is determined that the family's new life will be better than the one they left behind. Sequel to *Journey to America*.

5.7 Lowry, Lois. **Number the Stars.** Houghton Mifflin, 1989. ISBN 0-395-51060-0.

Ten years old in Copenhagen in 1943, Annemarie Johannsen hasn't had time to grow up yet, and now she's being asked to be brave when her family temporarily adopts Jewish Ellen to protect her from the Nazis. Annemarie's story tells us how the resistance to German occupation depended a great deal on individual, isolated acts of bravery during a time of great fear.

5.8 Pitts, Paul. **Racing the Sun.** Avon/Camelot Books, 1988. ISBN 0-380-75496-7.

Brandon knows very little about the Navajo culture of his family. His father left the reservation, changed his name from Redhouse to Rogers, and moved to a white suburb. Then when Brandon's grandfather becomes ill, he leaves his home on the reservation to come and live with his son's family. It is through this old man that Brandon learns the beauty and richness of his heritage.

5.9 Rochman, Hazel, compiler. **Somehow Tenderness Survives: Stories of Southern Africa.** Harper and Row, 1988. ISBN 0-06-025022-4.

Living in a society where racism is the rule might mean a number of things: hiding in a toilet every morning for fear of being discovered in the wrong neighborhood; watching your father being dragged from your home in the middle of the night; living in fear, depression, and hate. These ten stories and autobiographical accounts (five by black southern Africans and five by white southern Africans) explore the meaning of apartheid.

5.10 Roth-Hano, Renée. **Touch Wood: A Girlhood in Occupied France.** Four Winds Press, 1988. ISBN 0-02-777340-X.

In this novel based on her own childhood, the author describes the terror of World War II for French Jews. The oldest of three girls, Renée and her family flee her home in Alsace to safety in Paris. In Paris, though, the family watches as German soldiers take away more and more of their Jewish neighbors. In a desperate attempt to protect the girls, Renée's parents send them to a Catholic women's residence in Normandy. Separated from her parents for the first time, Renée realizes that this refuge, too, is in danger from the Nazis, and that she must help her sisters survive bombings that have moved dangerously close to them.

5.11 Tate, Eleanora E. **The Secret of Gumbo Grove.** Franklin Watts, 1987. ISBN 0-531-10298-X.

Raisin Stackhouse is intrigued by the mystery of what famous person is buried in the New Africa No. 1 Missionary Baptist Church Cemetery, which she is helping Miz Effie Pfluggins clean up. Through Miz Effie, Raisin learns about black history in Calvary County and learns some lessons about herself as well.

5.12 Wallin, Luke. **Ceremony of the Panther.** Bradbury Press, 1987. ISBN 0-02-792310-X.

Deep in the Florida Everglades, sixteen-year-old John Raincrow, a Miccosukee Indian, is caught between two paths. His father wants him to follow the path of tradition and become a Miccosukee shaman. His friends want him to join them in their pursuit of pleasure. John Raincrow struggles to find his own path.

5.13 Wisler, G. Clifton. **The Wolf's Tooth.** Lodestar Books, 1987. ISBN 0-525-67197-8.

Thirteen-year-old Elias Walsh isn't too happy about having to leave his home in Texas in order to move to the Indian reservation where his father will be the new school teacher. Life there is hard and playmates nonexistent until he meets Thomas Three Feathers, and the two boys decide to hunt the wolves that are killing the Walshes' chickens. Through this adventure, Elias earns Thomas's respect, and the boys develop a solid friendship and an understanding of each other's culture.

6 Family Life

6.1 Adler, C. S. **If You Need Me.** Macmillan, 1988. ISBN 0-02-700420-1.

As thirteen-year-old Lyn becomes closer to her stepmother, she realizes that her father seems to be drawing away from both of them. Lyn believes that Brian, the new boy next door, would be fun to know, but she becomes increasingly upset by the interest her father seems to be showing in Brian's mother. The two young people find themselves unable to stop a relationship that threatens to destroy both families.

6.2 Adler, C. S. **One Sister Too Many.** Macmillan, 1989. ISBN 0-02-700271-3.

Twelve-year-old Case is an individual. Outspoken and impulsive, she creates conflict at school and at home. She believes her teacher doesn't like her; the teacher believes Case is insolent and rebellious. Case believes her mother and stepfather don't love her; her parents believe that she could and should try harder. Case believes the babysitter recently hired for her younger sister is weird and untrustworthy; her parents believe—until it is almost too late—that Case simply overdramatizes. Sequel to *Split Sisters*.

6.3 Auch, Mary Jane. **Cry Uncle!** Holiday House, 1987. ISBN 0-8234-0660-1.

City-born Davey Anderson's new life on the farm proves to be a tough adjustment: his mother has discovered 101 ways to fix zucchini (so they don't waste the garden), and he is often the victim of bullying by the Spider twins. Then, as if things weren't bad enough, his seventy-four-year-old great-uncle comes to live with them, and Davey finds Uncle Will's slips into childhood behavior embarrassing and difficult to deal with.

6.4 Auch, Mary Jane. **Glass Slippers Give You Blisters.** Holiday House, 1989. ISBN 0-8234-0752-7.

Kelly is nervous about starting middle school, but her life begins to look up when she becomes involved with the school theater production of "Cinderella." Then her two best friends get parts and Kelly doesn't. She even gets kicked off the crew doing sets. Next, her grandmother has a stroke, and Kelly is pulled into the middle of a thirty-year conflict between her mother and her grandmother.

6.5 Auch, Mary Jane. **Pick of the Litter.** Holiday House, 1988. ISBN 0-8234-0692-X.

For eleven-year-old "Cat" Corwin, life is pretty easy as an only child. The fact that she was adopted has never bothered her because her parents have always said they were able to pick her. Then a drug helps Cat's mother get pregnant, possibly with more than one baby, and suddenly Cat's life no longer seems important to her parents as they prepare for children of their own.

6.6 Betancourt, Jeanne. **Home Sweet Home.** Bantam Books, 1988. ISBN 0-553-05469-4.

High school junior Tracy Jensen is thrown into culture shock when her parents move from New York City to her grandmother's farm. Most of the people she meets in her new rural school are kind, but ways are different there—perhaps less different, though, than they seem to Anya, a Russian exchange student also living in the tiny community. Together, Tracy and Anya endure Tracy's grandmother's stroke and try to raise enough money to help a family keep their farm. Fast friends, Tracy and Anya face cultural differences and life's drama together.

6.7 Boutis, Victoria. **Looking Out.** Four Winds Press, 1988. ISBN 0-02-711830-4.

In 1953 America has a kind of witch-hunt—a hunt for Communists. Ellen, whose family has just moved to a new town, must face the idea that her parents may be Communists. Ellen then must choose: her friends or her parents. Who is right? Or can there be another way?

6.8 Collier, James Lincoln. **Outside Looking In.** Macmillan, 1987. ISBN 0-02-723100-3.

Fourteen-year-old Fergy is tired of his family's lifestyle. He's tired of camping out and being dirty, but most of all he's afraid of growing up illiterate and of being branded a thief. His dad says it's all right to "reclaim" necessities from society, but Fergy no longer believes that. Fergy decides to run away, to try to find his grandparents, but he realizes that he cannot leave his little sister behind. He wants a normal life for both of them, but he hasn't considered that his little sister may not feel the same way he does.

6.9 Corcoran, Barbara. **You Put Up with Me, I'll Put Up with You.** Avon/Camelot Books, 1989. ISBN 0-380-70558-3.

When she is twelve, Kelly's life changes dramatically—and not for the better. She liked being an only child and living with her widowed mother. But now they are moving to her grandmother's old house so her mother can open a restaurant. If that's not bad enough, her mother's partners and their children will all be living in the same house, and Kelly will have to share a room with a boy-crazy cheerleader. Only her friendship with the strange girl next door and the prospect of a relationship with one of the older boys in the house might make life more tolerable, maybe even interesting.

6.10 Danziger, Paula. **Remember Me to Harold Square.** Laurel-Leaf Books, 1987. ISBN 0-440-20153-5.

Fourteen-year-old Kendra is worried about the boy who is coming to New York to live with her family for the summer. She is not excited about having to spend her summer with her little brother and this unknown boy. But when the three learn about the city-wide scavenger hunt that their parents have planned, the summer begins to look a little better. Can the three get along well enough to find everything and collect the special grand prize?

6.11 Dines, Carol. **Best Friends Tell the Best Lies.** Delacorte Press, 1989. ISBN 0-385-29704-1.

Best friends Leah and Tamara (one timid and one outrageous) are fourteen and live with their mothers. Their parents' divorces have been difficult for both of them. When Leah's mother becomes serious about her boyfriend José, Leah gets nasty, and with Tamara's help, tries to break them up. Leah viciously attacks José's heritage. But she does an about-face when she meets José's nephew, Miguel. He is great looking and talented, and he likes her, too. The electricity of first love, its frustration and pain, the confusion and insecurity of facing reality, and the discovery that a good friendship is not blind all help Leah to know and accept herself.

6.12 Ehrlich, Amy. **Where It Stops, Nobody Knows.** Dial Books for Young Readers, 1988. ISBN 0-8037-0575-1.

Thirteen-year-old Nina Lewis has moved from place to place with her mother all her life. They stop for a while in Vermont, where Nina plays on the basketball team and meets Sam, who might be her boyfriend. But over Nina's objections, she and her mother move again, to Utah and then to California. Once more having to give up a friend, Nina rebels, but they are on their way to New York. In New York, Nina, now sixteen, learns her mother's secret, and it changes her life forever.

6.13 Fine, Anne. **Alias Madame Doubtfire.** Joy Street Books, 1988. ISBN 0-316-28313-4.

Madame Doubtfire is Lydia, Christopher, and Natalie's babysitter. She's big and overdressed, and she has hairy, musclebound forearms. The children love her, but they fear the day when their divorced mother finds out why.

6.14 Fosburgh, Liza. **Cruise Control.** Bantam Books, 1988. ISBN 0-553-05491-0.

Gussie's mom used to be so much fun, but now all she does is sneak drinks in the pantry and rest upstairs in her bedroom. Gussie's dad, meanwhile, is very critical of Gussie, telling him how worthless and lazy he is. His sister Annie eats constantly, and brother Jimbo reads all the time to cope with the situation. Finally, Gussie can't stand things at home anymore, and he takes off for his uncle's house, where he discovers some startling things about his family.

6.15 Gaeddert, LouAnn. **A Summer Like Turnips.** Henry Holt, 1989. ISBN 0-8050-0839-X.

Bruce Hardy knows that his summer vacation in California won't be the same this year. After all, Gram is dead now. He's sure, though, that he and his good buddy Gramps will still have fun. What he finds, however, is that Gramps has changed in ways that scare him. Bruce's summer begins to look unbearable, until he meets Mac, Jenny, and Vanessa.

6.16 Graff, Nancy Price. **The Strength of the Hills: A Portrait of a Family Farm.** Photographs by Richard Howard. Little, Brown, 1989. ISBN 0-316-32277-6.

Family Life

This photo-and-text essay portrays one day of a fast-disappearing lifestyle. Generations of the Nelson family have lived on and worked the same land in Vermont for 170 years. Long days, hard work, and laughter are a part of the Nelson way of life as they work together, united in a common goal of keeping the land in the family.

6.17 Green, Connie Jordan. **The War at Home.** Margaret K. McElderry Books, 1989. ISBN 0-689-50470-5.

Mattie McDowell, thirteen, does not understand her family's move to Oak Ridge, Tennessee, during World War II. Her father is not permitted to discuss his job, and security regulations are very tight and rigidly enforced. As she begins to adjust to these changes, her cousin Virgil, a few months younger than she, comes to live with them. Now Mattie must also cope with Virgil's absolute belief in the superiority of males and with his monopolizing of her father.

6.18 Hahn, Mary Downing. **Following the Mystery Man.** Clarion Books, 1988. ISBN 0-89919-680-2.

When a mysterious stranger suddenly appears in her small town, Madigan Maloney convinces herself that he is the father she's never met. But when Madigan begins to explore the stranger's private life, she makes a dangerous discovery.

6.19 Hobbs, Will. **Changes in Latitudes.** Atheneum, 1988. ISBN 0-689-31385-3.

Things are changing for Travis, his sister Jennifer, and his brother Teddy: their mom is taking them to Mexico and their father is staying behind. When they get to Mexico, Travis wants to meet a gorgeous "fox," Teddy wants to see the beach where the endangered sea turtles nest, and Jennifer wants to do whatever is best for their family. What Travis and Teddy experience with the turtles affects them deeply, but not nearly so deeply as the tragedy that occurs to change their lives forever.

6.20 Husted, Darrell. **A Perfect Family.** British American, 1988. ISBN 0-945167-02-4.

On the surface, the Johnsons are a perfect middle-class American family. Bill works hard to see that his boys have the security he lacked in his own childhood, and his wife, Harriet, genuinely loves her sons. Beneath the surface, however, all is not well. Bill demands excellence, but he never listens. Harriet cannot handle any kind of confrontation. Of the three boys, Billy desperately tries to placate his father, Jo-jo turns to drugs, and Evan doesn't understand. Then, at Thanksgiving time, the entire family is murdered—except for the boy who pulls the trigger.

6.21 Jensen, Kathryn. **Pocket Change.** Macmillan, 1989. ISBN 0-02-747731-2.

Life is good to sixteen-year-old Josie. She is close to her father, genuinely likes her stepmother, and adores her baby brother. She also has a boyfriend who likes her very much. But then her father's behavior begins to change—he becomes moody, unpredictable, and frightening. When Josie realizes that his behavior can be traced to his experiences in the Vietnam War fifteen years earlier, she believes that she has the strength to help her dad and to keep the family together.

6.22 Jones, Rebecca C. **The Believers.** Arcade, 1989. ISBN 0-1-55970-035-1.

Tibby Taylor has "flair," although her teacher and principal might call it "disobedience." Tibby doesn't really care about school, but she does care about her glamorous TV-reporter mother, who never seems to have time to come home. What Tibby needs is a miracle, and when she comes in contact with a religious sect that claims particular kinds of power, Tibby believes that her miracle is at hand.

6.23 Klass, Sheila Solomon. **Credit-Card Carole.** Bantam Books, 1989. ISBN 0-553-27355-8.

Carole Warren's life seems to be falling apart. Her father has just announced that he is quitting dentistry to pursue a career in acting, and money will be tight. No more Saturdays shopping at the mall—and Carole's going to have to get a job. How will she be able to stand it?

6.24 Klass, Sheila Solomon. **Page Four.** Bantam Books, 1986. ISBN 0-553-26901-1.

David Smith is an all-American boy: intelligent, good-looking, athletic, and a straight-A student. He is close to his parents, who share his hopes for a prestigious college career. Then, in David's junior year, his dad leaves the family to begin a new life in Alaska with another woman, and David's and his mom's lives fall apart. Angry and shattered, David gives up on everything, but his mother's unhappiness and inactivity are tearing him apart. He must do something to help pull her through—but what?

6.25   Klein, Norma. **Now That I Know.** Bantam Books, 1988. ISBN 0-553-05472-4.

Nina's life is pretty good. Her parents are divorced, but that's not a problem; she divides her time between both houses. She wishes that her mother would get out more and that her father's friend Greg wouldn't hang around quite so much, but things at school are getting exciting, so she tries not to worry about it. She may become the editor of the school paper, and a very cute boy has some article ideas that he wants to share with her. But then Nina learns a family secret, and her world is suddenly turned upside down by problems she can't ignore.

6.26   Mahoney, Mary Reeves. **The Hurry-up Summer.** G. P. Putnam's Sons, 1987. ISBN 0-399-21430-5.

Life is changing too quickly for twelve-year-old Letitia "Letty" Lowe. First, Marfa, the woman who has taken care of Letty since she was little, moves away. Then Letty's father brings home a new girlfriend, and they want to send Letty to boarding school. Isn't life ever going to go Letty's way?

6.27   Marsden, John. **So Much to Tell You . . . .** Joy Street Books, 1987. ISBN 0-316-54877-4.

A year ago fourteen-year-old Marina quit talking. Now she's out of the hospital and enrolled in a school where her mother hopes she will learn to speak again. This novel, based on a true story, is Marina's diary. It is here that she reveals the tragic events that have pressed her into silence.

6.28   Naylor, Phyllis Reynolds. **The Year of the Gopher.** Bantam Books, 1988. ISBN 0-553-27131-8.

It's the end of George Richards's senior year, and everyone he knows has made plans to go to college—everyone but George. Against the wishes of his father and grandfather, both Harvard graduates, George decides to stay behind and work. He works at a variety of "gopher" jobs as he decides who he is and what to do with his life.

6.29 Paterson, Katherine. **Park's Quest.** Lodestar Books, 1988. ISBN 0-525-67258-3.

Park knows that his father was killed in Vietnam and that his mother refuses to talk about his father or say anything about his father's family. Determined to learn more, Park badgers his mother until she agrees to contact his father's family and ask if Park may visit. When Park arrives at his grandfather's home, he learns several family secrets and finally is able to account for his mother's reluctance to tell him anything.

6.30 Paulsen, Gary. **The Winter Room.** Orchard Books, 1989. ISBN 0-531-05839-5.

Life on a northern Minnesota farm is demanding, but for Eldon it is never monotonous. In the wintertime, Eldon likes evenings when the entire family gathers around the fire and listens to Uncle David tell stories of his long-dead Alida, or crazy Alen, or Viking conquerors. The stories forge a link between Eldon's world and the world beyond. Then one night Uncle David tells the story of the woodcutter, and Eldon's world will never be quite the same.

6.31 Pfeffer, Susan Beth. **Thea at Sixteen.** Bantam Books, 1988. ISBN 0-553-05498-8.

Thea Sebastian is sick of being ordered around by her father, but she also hates it when he is angry with her, so she agrees to volunteer at a nearby hospital to please him. It is there that she meets Gloria, a twelve-year-old girl dying of cancer, and Kip, Gloria's eighteen-year-old brother. Through her relationship with these two people, Thea finds the strength to stand up to her father and learns to love and respect herself and her family. Part of The Sebastian Sisters series.

6.32 Pfeffer, Susan Beth. **The Year without Michael.** Bantam Books, 1987. ISBN 0-553-05430-9.

The already troubled Chapman family is plunged into a nightmare when fourteen-year-old Michael mysteriously disappears. His seventeen-year-old sister, Jodi, watches her remaining family fall apart as they desperately help police search for Michael. Finding him seems the only way to save her family, and Jodi finally risks her own life to find Michael among runaways and pimps on the streets of New York City.

Family Life

6.33 Rodowsky, Colby. **Fitchett's Folly.** Farrar, Straus and Giroux, 1987. ISBN 0-374-32342-9.

When Sarey's father, keeper of a lifesaving station, is killed trying to save the passengers on a wrecked ship, Sarey is very upset. Then, even as Sarey's father is buried beside her mother's grave, Sarey's Aunt-Mama takes in Faith Wilkinson, orphaned by the shipwreck. Sarey sees Faith as not only an intruder but the reason her father died. Feeling miserable and hateful, Sarey acts out her anger. So many awful things happen, it seems that nothing worse can. Then Faith's life is in danger, and Sarey makes a decision that changes her life and chases away her fear.

6.34 Rylant, Cynthia. **A Kindness.** Orchard Books, 1988. ISBN 0-531-05767-4.

For all of his fifteen years, Chip and his mother have been a family. Chip's father left them to go to a new life in Australia, and mother and son have formed a close relationship. Suddenly that closeness is threatened when Chip's mother tells him that she is pregnant but won't tell him who the baby's father is. Because his mother decides to have—and keep—the baby, Chip must come to grips with his own feelings about his mother, who he feels has betrayed him; his new little sister, whom he does not want; an unnamed, unseen father, whom Chip sees as gutless; and perhaps most of all, himself.

6.35 Scariano, Margaret. **Summer Strike Out.** Illustrated by Matthew Gouig. High Noon Books, 1988. ISBN 0-87879-617-7.

Sue has the perfect summer planned. She's going to work at Whipple's Fix-it Shop, pitch on the softball team, and save her money for car insurance. Then her cranky Grandma Ellis arrives to stay with them after a serious illness. Suddenly, Sue finds herself in the role of babysitter for a mean old lady who can't talk and is confined to a wheelchair. Her summer looks ruined.

6.36 Shannon, George. **Unlived Affections.** Harper and Row, 1989. ISBN 0-06-025304-5.

Seventeen-year-old Willie has lived with his grandmother as long as he can remember. His mother died in a car accident, and his grandmother told him that his father died before Willie was born, but she absolutely refused to tell him any more than that. After her death, Willie is left to get her things ready for auction and then go off to college. When he cleans out his mother's room, a room his grandmother had never let him enter, he discovers a box of letters from his father. As the letters show him the father he has never known, they also reveal some family secrets.

6.37 Singer, Marilyn. **Several Kinds of Silence.** Harper and Row, 1988. ISBN 0-06-025627-3.

Franny Yeager faces several problems. Her much-loved grandmother suffers from diabetes and often refuses to take care of herself. Franny's dad is struggling to keep his job and angry about the prospect of being laid off without warning. The only thing that keeps Franny going is her job at a florist's shop, a job she really likes. Then she meets Ren, a boy to whom she is definitely attracted—and one she knows her parents will disapprove of.

6.38 Snyder, Carol. **Leave Me Alone, Ma.** Bantam Books, 1987. ISBN 0-553-27591-7.

Fourteen-year-old Jaimie Newman lives with her mother, father, and grandmother. Lately she feels as though she and her grandmother are alone; her parents are always out of town on business. Jaimie does have other things to keep her busy, though, like entering the sculpture competition at school, helping a new friend who is homeless, and trying to get her best friend's brother to notice her.

6.39 Weller, Frances Ward. **Boat Song.** Macmillan, 1987. ISBN 0-02-792611-7.

The strange music that eleven-year-old Jonno hears on the beach seems to be coming from somewhere in the fog. Hurt that his father doesn't seem to care about him, Jonno searches for the music and finds Rob, a colorful Scottish bagpiper. Old enough to be Jonno's grandfather, Rob remembers what it's like to be a kid and even reads Jonno's thoughts. Their relationship enables Jonno to look more closely at his family.

7 Fantasy

7.1 Banks, Lynne Reid. **The Fairy Rebel.** Illustrated by William Geldart. Doubleday, 1988. ISBN 0-385-24483-5.

The world of enchantment and the world of people rarely meet, but when they do—look out! Humans Jan and Charlie have always wanted a baby, and Tiki, the blue jeans–wearing fairy, has always needed to challenge the Fairy Queen in little ways. By granting Jan her wish, Tiki turns mischief into rebellion and endangers herself, her human friends, and her fairy-child creation.

7.2 Charnas, Suzy McKee. **The Bronze King.** Bantam Books, 1988. ISBN 0-553-27104-0.

After Valentine Marsh hears the explosion inside of the New York City subway station, strange items begin to disappear—like the statue of Jagiello in Central Park. Then, when the Princes of Darkness launch an attack on her, she meets Paavo Latvela and, later, his friend Joel. Together they begin the battle against the Kraken, which threatens to swallow the world with its evil.

7.3 Charnas, Suzy McKee. **The Silver Glove.** Bantam Books, 1988. ISBN 0-553-05470-8.

Valentine Marsh has always been aware of her Granny Gran's special powers; however, when Granny Gran escapes from the retirement home and sends Valli a silver glove through the telephone wires, Valli isn't sure what to expect next. Then she finds out that her school psychologist is really an evil wizard who has come to Earth to steal human souls, and Gran and Valli must use the glove to defeat him. This will be hard to do, since the wizard is dating Valli's mother.

7.4 Dexter, Catherine. **Mazemaker.** Morrow Junior Books, 1989. ISBN 0-688-07383-2.

Twelve-year-old Minnie discovers a maze spray-painted on the asphalt of the deserted schoolyard and decides to solve it. However, when she gets to the center of the maze, the landscape around her collapses, and she is hurled backward in time into the nineteenth century. Now, only the person who painted the maze can help her, and Minnie sets out on a confusing search to find this mysterious figure.

7.5 Furlong, Monica. **Wise Child.** Alfred A. Knopf, 1987. ISBN 0-394-99105-2.

Abandoned by her mother, Maeve, a black witch, nine-year-old Wise Child is publicly auctioned and taken in by Juniper, the healer and mysterious sorceress who lives outside their remote Scottish village. With Juniper's care, spoiled Wise Child begins to grow and learn—until Maeve reappears. Caught in the whirlwind between Juniper and Maeve, Wise Child discovers her own magical power and then must decide on her future.

7.6 Garden, Nancy. **The Door Between.** Farrar, Straus and Giroux, 1987. ISBN 0-374-31833-6.

Melissa Dunn is told by Fours Crossing's oldest citizen that she must once more stop the evil hermit and his wild dogs from destroying the town. Although her last encounter with the hermit almost ended in her death, Melissa faces the challenges the hermit sends her way, all the while knowing that to win this time, she will have to go through the door to the Otherworld. Part of the Fours Crossing series.

7.7 Halam, Ann. **Transformations.** Orchard Books, 1988. ISBN 0-531-05766-6.

Anything or anyone can be changed—sometimes to good, sometimes to evil. When the magical covener, Zanne, comes to the closed, cold-hearted society of Minith, she finds an entire people who are changing. But they hide the secret of how and why, and if Zanne cannot discover the secret in time, their whole world could be wickedly transformed.

7.8 Henry, Maeve. **The Witch King.** Orchard Books, 1988. ISBN 0-531-05738-0.

Robert knows which stories are true—the ones told him by the old witch woman, not the ones about the Spell told in the royal city. But even if its story is false, the Spell does have power—an evil power—over Robert, his wizard friend Godfrey, the beautiful Princess Sophie, and her brother, Prince David. Despite his mistakes and their terrible cost, Robert must try to release the magical truth and discover his destiny.

Fantasy

7.9 Jacques, Brian. **Redwall.** Illustrated by Gary Chalk. Philomel Books, 1986. ISBN 0-399-21424-0.

Cluny the Scourge and his evil army of rats, weasels, and ferrets are moving to attack the peace-loving creatures who live in Redwall Abbey. Not since the ancient times of the mighty hero, Martin the Warrior, have the mice had to defend their beloved abbey. The novice, Matthias, and the old and wise Methuselah attempt to unravel the riddles surrounding the lost, legendary sword of Martin, but can they do so in time to protect the abbey from the wicked forces of Cluny?

7.10 Johnson, Norma Tadlock. **Bats on the Bedstead.** Illustrated by Judith Gwyn Brown. Avon/Camelot Books, 1988. ISBN 0-380-70540-0.

The Engstrom family has just moved to an old house in the country. Ricky, the older of the two boys, is awakened at night by Voro, the bat ringleader, who threatens Ricky and tells him his family must leave the house. No one else sees these bats, not even Ricky's younger brother who shares a room with Ricky. When Ricky tells his parents about the bats, they take him to a psychologist for counseling. Was Ricky crazy, or were there bats on the bedstead?

7.11 Logan, Carolyn F. **The Power of the Rellard.** Margaret K. McElderry Books, 1986. ISBN 0-689-50445-4.

For Lucy, Georgie, and Shelley, a fantasy game they played while Lucy was sick turns into a real-life battle between the powers of good and evil. In the game, Lucy passed the twelve trials and became the Keeper of the Rellard; however, she is soon the real-life target of evil disguised as people she knows. Soon Lucy, Georgie, and Shelley are battling to survive against cold, fire, floods, and tornadoes.

7.12 McGowen, Tom. **The Magician's Company.** Lodestar Books, 1988. ISBN 0-525-67261-3.

Three thousand years from now, intelligent, mutated rats are plotting to destroy humanity. They call themselves the Reen. When the magician Armidor, his apprentice Tigg, and puppeteer Julia warn the High Chairman, he ignores them, and Armidor, Tigg, and Julia are left to stop the Reen on their own. Sequel to *The Magician's Apprentice*.

7.13 McKenzie, Ellen Kindt. **Kashka.** Henry Holt, 1987. ISBN 0-8050-0327-4.

Mischievous but lively and good-hearted, the young court acrobat and musician Kashka finds his playful life changed when he learns of a scheme that might give the sorceress Lady Ysene power over all of the Kingdom of Darai. Using Princess Ekama in her magic, Lady Ysene, plotting with her evil brother, the Lord of Xon, seems to be achieving her goal. Soon, Kashka realizes that only he can save the kingdom.

7.14 Moulton, Deborah. **The First Battle of Morn.** Dial Books, 1988. ISBN 0-8037-0550-6.

Torin has dreams that show him the fate of his planet, Morn. When he is instructed to move to the city of the Teachers with his flying horse Saba, those dreams thrust him into the center of the struggle for his planet. The Teachers want him as their "mind child," and the rebels want him as their savior. What will Torin do?

7.15 Posner, Richard. **Sparrow's Flight.** M. Evans, 1988. ISBN 0-87131-544-0.

Sixteen-year-old Julie Hoffman's father left when she was twelve. At her new high school, Julie begins to write a book—an imaginary quest for her father and a mission to destroy the mother she struggles against. When she has a chance to actually accomplish both, Julie must make a hard decision.

7.16 Price, Susan. **The Ghost Drum: A Cat's Tale.** Farrar, Straus and Giroux, 1987. ISBN 0-374-32538-3.

In a country hidden in darkness half the year and buried under a crust of cold, white snow, lives Safa, son of Czar Guidon. His evil fortune-telling aunt and his greedy father have locked Safa in a tower. No one, except the witch-girl Chingis, cares that Safa weeps in his prison; only Chingis, with a ghost drum and a skull, has the power to confront her own chilling fear and rescue Safa.

7.17 Rodda, Emily. **The Pigs Are Flying!** Illustrated by Noela Young. Greenwillow Books, 1988. ISBN 0-688-08130-4.

Rachel's adventure begins on a rainy Saturday morning. Bored with having a cold and tired of staying in bed, she suddenly finds herself transported out of her room and riding a unicorn through a strange place where storms cause pigs to float and other unlikely events to occur. In this strange place, Rachel is an outsider. Will she ever be able to find her way home again?

7.18 Seidler, Tor. **The Tar Pit.** Michael di Capua Books, 1987. ISBN 0-374-37383-3.

Edward Small, Jr., doesn't get along well at home or at school, but he does get along well with an allosaurus—his imaginary friend Alexander. Whenever Edward calls or needs help, Alexander comes to his rescue, often in a gory way. Eventually, Alexander and another older allosaurus help Edward to gain acceptance.

7.19 Selden, George. **The Old Meadow.** Illustrated by Garth Williams. Farrar, Straus and Giroux, 1987. ISBN 0-374-35616-5.

The town council of Hedley, Connecticut, has declared the Old Meadow a historical landmark and has decided that old Mr. Budd and his dog Dubber must move. However, Old Meadow is also home to many animals who feel that it would not be the same without Mr. Budd and Dubber. The animals decide to help, but what can such a diverse group of woodland and meadow creatures accomplish in opposition to the human inhabitants of Hedley?

7.20 Service, Pamela F. **Winter of Magic's Return.** Fawcett Juniper Books, 1987. ISBN 0-449-70202-2.

Five hundred years after the nuclear nightmare, the winter world of magic and mutants begins to thaw. Two young friends, Wally and Heather, choose to begin a journey that might help their mysterious friend Earl discover who he once was. In the process, they discover who they themselves are—and the magic and cost of friendship.

7.21 Wells, Rosemary. **Through the Hidden Door.** Illustrated by author. Dial Books for Young Readers, 1987. ISBN 0-8037-0276-0.

Barney Pennimen has been accused of breaking the rules at Winchester Boys' Academy. Part of his punishment is to spend time in the library doing research on world disasters. While he is there one day, he finds a younger boy, Snowy Cobb, also doing some research. Snowy convinces Barney that he has made a significant discovery in a cave nearby but that he needs some help. The two boys uncover some ancient relics in the cave, but they don't want to tell anyone else about them. They also discover that Barney's former friends and the new headmaster are very dangerous people.

7.22　Yolen, Jane. **The Faery Flag: Stories and Poems of Fantasy and the Supernatural.** Orchard Books, 1989. ISBN 0-531-05838-7.

In one story, the "retired" wolves at the Happy Dens Rest Home tell Nurse Lamb that they were victims of bad press, and they give the real scoop about themselves, Red Riding Hood, and Peter. In contrast to this humorous "old wolves' tale" is "Wolf Child," an eerie story about a ghost in an Indian jungle. The ghost eats people. The villagers know it, but the occupying British soldiers do not believe it. There is also a she-wolf with five cubs, who has difficulty finding them enough to eat. There is suspense and the unexpected. Seven other tales and seven poems filled with magic, wonder, and horror make this a collection to be read again and again.

7.23　Yolen, Jane. **A Sending of Dragons.** Laurel-Leaf Books, 1987. ISBN 0-440-20309-0.

Jakkin, the young Pit Master, and his friend Akki have agreed not to take any chances after they've been chased into the mountains with their five dragon hatchlings. The revolutionary forces soon close in on them, however, and they must take refuge in a cave. Little do Jakkin and Akki realize that they will be pulled deeper into the caves and into a captivity difficult to escape. Book 3 of the Pit Dragons series.

7.24　Zelazny, Roger. **Sign of Chaos.** Avon Books, 1988. ISBN 0-380-89637-0.

Since the young sorcerer Merlin is a prince of the royal family of Amber, he rarely gets a chance to use his magic. This changes when Merlin's half-brother Jurt teams up with the evil magician Mask to seize the most powerful fortress in Amber. Merlin confronts the two wizards at the Keep of the Four Worlds in a thrilling duel of magic. Book 8 in the Amber series.

8 Folklore and Legends

8.1 Babbitt, Natalie. **The Devil's Other Storybook.** Illustrated by author. Michael di Capua Books, 1987. ISBN 0-374-31767-4.

The Devil in this collection of tales is a rather likable creature who is bested by Colombine, a parrot, and by Akbar, a camel. However, he also proves himself as clever as ever with a trio of pompous ladies on the River Styx and with a big-game hunter condemned to forever hunt a rhino with a hole in its nose.

8.2 Lester, Julius. **More Tales of Uncle Remus: Further Adventures of Brer Rabbit, His Friends, Enemies, and Others.** Illustrated by Jerry Pinkney. Dial Books, 1988. ISBN 0-8037-0419-4.

Always getting in and out of trouble—that's Brer Rabbit. This pack of illustrated tales about the Trickster, "the cunning one" who lives in all of us, follows Brer Rabbit as he wanders around the countryside, getting in and out of mischief.

8.3 McKinley, Robin. **The Outlaws of Sherwood.** Greenwillow Books, 1988. ISBN 0-688-07178-3.

According to legend, Robin Hood was a former nobleman who became an outlaw in twelfth-century England. He and his band of merry men lived in Sherwood Forest and stole from the rich and gave to the poor. They were famous for not hurting anyone. The exciting adventures of Robin Hood, Maid Marian, Friar Tuck, Little John, and the rest are retold here.

8.4 Norman, Howard. **"How Glooskap Outwits the Ice Giants" and Other Tales of the Maritime Indians.** Illustrated by Michael McCurdy. Joy Street Books, 1989. ISBN 0-316-61181-6.

Long, long ago Glooskap, a mythical giant, roamed the east coast of New England and Canada. Six tales relate his adventures in pitting his power against the forces of nature and evil. A part of the rich storytelling tradition of the Maritime Indians, Glooskap stories taught people how to live and how to overcome obstacles.

9 Friendship

9.1 Betancourt, Jeanne. **Not Just Party Girls.** Bantam Books, 1989. ISBN 0-553-05497-X.

Anne Paley, Kate Rice, and Janet Bates are successful sixteen-year-old professionals who present theme parties for kids and in between are planning for college and a trip to Europe together. Their close friendship is tested when Anne has doubts about her lifestyle after a stint working with poor migrants, and Kate and Janet experience family problems. Each girl is distracted by her own frustration and pain. Can they find a way to continue their friendship and their business?

9.2 Blume, Judy. **Just as Long as We're Together.** Orchard Books, 1987. ISBN 0-531-05729-1.

The first year of junior high is a tough adjustment for most, but for Stephanie it is really hard. Her parents are having big marriage problems, and Stephanie doesn't feel as if she has anyone to share her fears with. Then, when Rachel, her best friend since second grade, becomes good friends with Alison, a girl who has just moved from California, Stephanie feels left out and totally alone.

9.3 Cross, Gillian. **A Map of Nowhere.** Holiday House, 1989. ISBN 0-8234-0741-1.

When Nick finds schoolmate Joseph Fisher's lost wallet in his bookbag, he also finds a note about monsters and underground dragons. Interested in Dungeons and Dragons himself, Nick is determined to join in Joseph's mysterious game, although the two boys—and their two families—are very different. When Nick discovers who put the wallet in his bookbag and why, the game takes a mysterious turn, and Nick must decide where his responsibilities and loyalties lie.

9.4 Ethridge, Kenneth E. **Viola, Furgy, Bobbi, and Me.** Holiday House, 1989. ISBN 0-8234-0746-2.

Ninth-grader Stephen White becomes best friends with seventy-eight-year-old Detroit Tigers fan Viola Spencer. When Viola's two middle-aged daughters, "Wicked Witch" and "Plastic Smile," attempt to put her in a nursing home, Stephen, his girlfriend Bobbi, and his eccentric friend Furgy work to help her.

9.5 Gibbons, Faye. **King Shoes and Clown Pockets.** Morrow Junior Books, 1989. ISBN 0-688-06592-9.

Everything stacks up against Raymond Brock. His family is poor, his parents don't have time for him, his brother and sister think he's a pest, he's terribly shy, and he gets everyone's hand-me-downs. Moving to a new town and a new school terrifies Ray until he discovers a friend, Bruce Manis, the son of the local junk dealer. Bruce is brash, independent, and seemingly carefree. Together Ray and Bruce explore, sharing adventures, secrets, and a very special dog.

9.6 Gondosch, Linda. **Who's Afraid of Haggerty House?** Illustrated by Helen Cogancherry. Lodestar Books, 1987. ISBN 0-525-67198-6.

Sixth-grader Kelly McCoy has a big fight with her two best friends. In order to fill the void, Kelly develops a friendship with old Mrs. Haggerty, who lives in a haunted house. During the time Kelly spends with Mrs. Haggerty, she learns a great deal about friendship and about ghosts.

9.7 Hoppe, Joanne. **Pretty Penny Farm.** William Morrow, 1987. ISBN 0-688-07201-1.

Fifteen-year-old Beth Bridgewater is having the perfect summer in New Hampshire at Pretty Penny Farm. Dave Fuller, a college boy, is taking her out, and she's getting to train his beautiful chestnut stallion, Charmin'. She is even becoming friends with Sophie Chmielewski, the unpopular girl her mom invited to join them for the summer. Then Beth and Charmin' win a horse race, and Beth suddenly finds herself involved with criminals.

9.8 Klein, Norma. **My Life as a Body.** Alfred A. Knopf, 1987. ISBN 0-394-89051-5.

Augie Lloyd, a high school senior in New York City, has misgivings about tutoring new student Sam Feldman, paralyzed from the waist down after an automobile accident. They seem so different: Sam was an athlete, is extremely wealthy, and is slow to speak after his accident; Augie is an artist who reads a lot of literature and is very intelligent. Sam has had several girlfriends and has experienced the physical side of life; Augie has not. Can two such seemingly opposite people find anything on which to build a friendship?

9.9 Pinsker, Judith. **A Lot Like You.** Bantam Books, 1988. ISBN 0-553-05445-7.

Howard Nevelson is two years older than Bo Barett, and he's also a member of the "in" crowd at Parkview High. Bo has a crush on Howard because he is the one person at school who has never made her feel bad about being overweight. Then when Howard's mother dies in a car accident, Howard changes, and no one at school knows how to act around him—no one except Bo, that is. She decides to do whatever she can to help him.

9.10 Rostkowski, Margaret I. **The Best of Friends.** Harper and Row, 1989. ISBN 0-06-025104-2.

Dan is a perfectionist driven to even higher performance by his demanding father. Sarah, Dan's younger sister, is active in an anti–Vietnam War group even though she knows her stand will infuriate her father. Will, Dan's best friend, has been content to live in Dan's shadow, allowing Dan to make decisions for them both. Now, as graduation nears and the Vietnam War more directly affects their lives, each of the three must make some very important decisions, decisions that will alter their lives—and their friendship.

9.11 Spinelli, Jerry. **Dump Days.** Little, Brown, 1988. ISBN 0-316-80706-0.

J. D. Kidd and Duke Pickwell are best buddies. With sixth grade just over, they are making stupendous plans for the perfect summer day. To make money for their dream day, they plan wild get-rich schemes and earn cash by rounding up four-year-old Erin, who escapes her mom before getting dressed; by rescuing a storekeeper from a rat; and by holding an extravaganza of a World's Fair. But when J.D. and Duke disagree about how to handle a problem, their friendship is on the line. With the help of a neighbor, they find that their perfect day really happens—although in a completely unexpected way.

9.12 Zalben, Jane Breskin. **Water from the Moon.** Farrar, Straus and Giroux, 1987. ISBN 0-374-38238-7.

Nicole Bernstein is an average sixteen year old: she likes art and good food, thinks about boys, and prefers to be called Nicky. She is intrigued by the new student, Tanya, though her best friend Amy warns her to stay away from Tanya. Her other intrigue is Josh Brent, a senior at NYU who works for her dad. Nicole and Tanya cut class one day to go see Josh—an experience which leads to important discoveries about herself and her expectations and perceptions of other people.

10 Growing Up

10.1 Behrens, Michael. **At the Edge.** Avon/Flare Books, 1988. ISBN 0-380-75610-2.

The seventeen-year-old author of this book makes the main character, Dan Shallot, come alive as he faces the challenges of accepting his parents' divorce, dealing with his manic-depressive girlfriend, and living up to the expectations of his swimming coach. Eventually, Dan is forced to make some decisions that will affect his entire future.

10.2 Bell, William. **Crabbe's Journey.** Little, Brown, 1986. ISBN 0-316-08837-4.

Franklin Crabbe, a senior from a wealthy family, has always done well in school and has always played by the rules. However, just before finals, he is hopelessly frustrated with everything. He plans an escape into the wilderness, where mishap brings him into contact with the most influential person in his life, a woman who teaches him about wilderness survival and about himself. But he can't stay with her forever, and leaving is one of the hardest things he's ever done.

10.3 Block, Francesca Lia. **Weetzie Bat.** Harper and Row, 1989. ISBN 0-06-020534-2.

Weetzie Bat hates high school because students seem to be so unaware. She and Dirk, her gay best friend, want to live "happily ever after," but long-range happiness eludes them. Given a cottage by Dirk's grandmother, they also locate the companions they have searched for; but the glitz of the pop culture that is their environment cannot protect them from the despair at a world of disease and unhappiness. Yet, when their illusions are destroyed, they conclude that people can *choose* love in order to live happily, for now, if not ever after.

10.4 Bottner, Barbara. **Let Me Tell You Everything: Memoirs of a Lovesick Intellectual.** Harper and Row, 1989. ISBN 0-06-020596-2.

When a gorgeous new teacher takes over her advanced social studies class, Brogan Arthur worries that her feminist ideals may melt. She does everything she can to impress him—short of throwing herself at his feet—but he seems to only have eyes for Rosanna Dakis, the brown-eyed bombshell of the senior class. Articulate and intelligent to the last, Brogan deals with this unrequited love the same way she deals with her alcoholic father—by coming up with theories and helping others.

10.5   Boyd, Candy Dawson. **Charlie Pippin.** Macmillan, 1987. ISBN 0-02-726350-9.

Charlie Pippin, at eleven, is an enterprising young businesswoman. However, her principal says that school is not an appropriate place for Charlie to set up shop, and her father is furious with her. As Charlie struggles to understand her father, she learns that he has not always been so easily angered, so willing to take offense. Fighting in Vietnam changed him, but no one will tell Charlie what happened or even what the war in Vietnam was all about. She will have to find out those things for herself.

10.6   Busselle, Rebecca. **Bathing Ugly.** Orchard Books, 1988. ISBN 0-531-05801-8.

After the summer camp director, Miss Mack, orders Betsy onto the old white scale and announces that she needs to lose weight, Betsy becomes painfully aware that what her mother has called baby fat is *real* fat. Determined to change her body, Betsy makes herself a goal to be slim enough to enter the end-of-camp Bathing Beauty Contest. No one, not even her friends, dreams how far Betsy will go to be a bathing beauty, or just how powerful an ending Betsy's summer will have.

10.7   Butler, Bonnie. **Dreaming.** Fawcett Juniper Books, 1987. ISBN 0-449-70142-5.

Although Lois Nestlerod may appear hostile and unattractive, on the inside there is a different Lois. This Lois longs for one thing: someone, anyone, to love her.

10.8   Calvert, Patricia. **Stranger, You and I.** Avon/Flare Books, 1987. ISBN 0-380-70600-8.

Hughie wants to be another Ernest Hemingway and get out of his small Illinois hometown as fast as possible. But there are complications. Zee, his best friend since fourth grade, has become a stranger and won't talk to him. And all of a sudden, Hughie notices that his parents and little brother are real people and need his help. Hughie has to grow up fast.

10.9 Carkeet, David. **The Silent Treatment.** Harper and Row, 1988. ISBN 0-06-020978-X.

Ricky Appleton, fifteen, and his friend Nate are determined to solve this year's Sierra Days Gold Rush mystery. If they succeed, they will win $2,000—and they will defeat Cindy Cargill, Ricky's main competitor and—very possibly—main interest. While they look for clues, Ricky must also learn to cope with the silence at home—silence from his father, who uses it as a weapon to keep order, and silence from his mother, who says nothing in order to keep the peace.

10.10 Christiansen, C. B. **A Small Pleasure.** Avon/Flare Books, 1989. ISBN 0-380-70699-7.

Things just don't happen to you in a small town, not big things, anyway—not unless you make them happen. So Wray Jean develops a three-year plan to be smarter, more popular, and cuter. Things don't always go according to plan, however, and Wray Jean discovers that even when people get what they want, they find that maybe that isn't what they really wanted after all.

10.11 Cole, Brock. **Celine.** Farrar, Straus and Giroux, 1989. ISBN 0-374-31234-6.

Celine is a not-very-happy sixteen-year-old artist. Left with her twenty-two-year-old stepmother while her father is on a lecture tour, Celine believes the world has conspired against her. Her teacher rejects her essay on Holden Caulfield and demands a rewrite. She gets stuck with the neighbor's kid for the weekend. Her boyfriend wants more attention than she wants to give him. However, unless she "shows a little maturity," she will not be allowed a summer visit to Italy—a visit from which she plans not to return.

10.12 Cole, Brock. **The Goats.** Farrar, Straus and Giroux, 1987. ISBN 0-374-32678-9.

The "goats," a boy and a girl, are stripped of their clothes and left on an island for the night by the other kids—a tradition and annual prank at the summer camp where they are staying. Reluctant to be spied upon during the night and then found on the island in the morning, the two "goats" manage to escape. Rather than return to camp, though, they decide to run away and scare the camp counselors into thinking that something has happened to them.

10.13 Cooney, Caroline B. **Among Friends.** Bantam Books, 1987. ISBN 0-553-05446-5.

Six high school juniors are asked by their English teacher to keep a diary for three months. Emily, Hilary, Paul, Jennie, Ansley, and Jared all seem to have so much going for them; yet each believes that someone else's life is perfect. The diary entries reflect conflict, success, jealousy, friendship, rivalry, insecurity, and, throughout, the ability or inability to cope.

10.14 Corcoran, Barbara. **The Hideaway.** Avon/Flare Books, 1989. ISBN 0-380-70635-0.

When their drunk driving accident paralyzes a newspaperman, Tom takes the blame for his friend Buddy, who was driving. After Tom is locked up in a school for delinquent boys, he decides to escape and find Buddy so they can make up a story to get Tom out of trouble. But what Tom finds is not at all what he expects.

10.15 Currey, Richard. **Fatal Light.** E. P. Dutton/Seymour Lawrence, 1988. ISBN 0-525-24622-3.

A young man is eighteen years old and a high school senior in 1967. Although he plans on getting an athletic scholarship and going to college, a change in draft classification sends him to Vietnam instead. A medic there, he finds himself caught up in the horror of war and the task of caring for the wounded, the dying, and the dead. When he returns to the United States, he finds that nothing will ever be the same; he has "lost his own time."

10.16 Daneman, Meredith. **Francie and the Boys.** Delacorte Press, 1988. ISBN 0-440-50137-7.

Thirteen-year-old Francie is shocked when she's given a chance to perform in a play at a London boys' school. She lacks experience with drama and with boys, but as the play proceeds, her talents shine through both success and failure. More importantly, though, she learns to identify the difference between true friends and people who only play the role.

10.17 Davis, Jenny. **Sex Education.** Orchard Books, 1988. ISBN 0-531-05756-9.

Mrs. Fulton plans to change the biology curriculum and devote the first semester to sex education. The major assignment for the term is a "caring project." Livvie and David agree that because they care deeply for each other they will do their project together. They choose a young couple who have just moved into the subdivision, but the project demands far more of them than anyone expected or wanted.

10.18 Feuer, Elizabeth. **One Friend to Another.** Farrar, Straus and Giroux, 1987. ISBN 0-374-35642-4.

When she changes schools in seventh grade, Nicole Aldrich is thrilled at the chance to change her image from "the Brain" to one more popular. Her efforts to put forth a new image seem successful when Rhonda Winkler, one of the most popular girls in school, befriends her, and she falls in love with a California boy. But someone betrays Nicole, and she is humiliated and embarrassed in front of the entire student body. Feeling inferior and helpless, Nicole must either betray herself or discover who betrayed her.

10.19 French, Michael. **Us against Them.** Bantam Books, 1987. ISBN 0-553-27647-6.

Sixteen-year-old Reed, the leader of a club with a reputation for bucking adult authority, decides to show adults he doesn't need them by taking his friends camping in the Adirondacks. The trip starts out just fine, but the group soon begins to fall apart, and then each person is forced to choose between loyalty to friends and his or her own conscience.

10.20 George, Jean Craighead. **Shark beneath the Reef.** Harper and Row, 1989. ISBN 0-06-021992-0.

The Mexican government is working to force small fishermen out of business, and young Tomás Torrez must decide whether to become a fisherman and work to save his family now or to continue his education and work to help his people later. When he comes face to face with a shark, the most-prized catch for fishermen of the Sea of Cortez, Tomás also comes face to face with the decision of his life.

10.21 Hall, Lynn. **The Leaving.** Collier Books, 1988. ISBN 0-02-043310-7.

Like her mother, Roxanne loves her life on the farm. But growing up seems to demand that she leave—and lose—everything she cherishes: her horse, her friends, the land. It takes a job in the big city to help Roxanne discover that leaving can be a way of coming home.

10.22 Hinton, S. E. **Taming the Star Runner.** Delacorte Press, 1988. ISBN 0-440-50058-3.

After attempting to kill his stepfather, sixteen-year-old Travis Harris is sent to Oklahoma to live with his uncle. Travis feels he doesn't belong in this small hick town where no one realizes how cool he is. But then he gets his novel published, falls in love with Casey Kencaide, and begins to see a parallel between himself and a stubborn horse named Star Runner.

10.23 Holl, Kristi D. **Hidden in the Fog.** Atheneum, 1989. ISBN 0-689-31494-9.

Thirteen-year-old Nikki Lynd lives on a Mississippi riverboat that has been converted to a hotel. Run by her parents and two other families, the hotel seems the realization of many dreams, especially those of Nikki's father. Then hard times hit, and the families face losing not only their dreams but their livelihoods as well. Nikki decides that she must come to the rescue; however, along with her desire to save the situation comes anger over being saddled with the responsibility for her parents' problems.

10.24 Holl, Kristi D. **No Strings Attached.** Atheneum, 1988. ISBN 0-689-31399-3.

June Finch's mom is recovering from bleeding ulcers and June's foster grandfather, Franklin, doesn't fit in at the retirement home where he is living, so June decides that she, her mom, and Franklin should all live together in Franklin's house. Franklin, however, is very blunt and quite often crabby, and June finds herself having a difficult time adjusting to her new family and to her first year of junior high school.

10.25 Hooper, Nancy J. **Carrie's Games.** Avon/Flare Books, 1987. ISBN 0-380-70538-9.

Carrie, a junior in high school, has always been pampered by her older brothers and her father and is used to having things her way. When she feels threatened by her father's growing interest in his new secretary, Carrie decides to divert his attention by dating Tony, who is just the right guy to worry her father. But Carrie fails to consider the feelings of Matt, her boyfriend, and Sarah, her best friend and Matt's twin sister. Eventually Carrie finds that manipulating other people does not always work as planned.

10.26 Jones, Robin D. **No Shakespeare Allowed.** Atheneum, 1989. ISBN 0-689-31488-4.

Portia Cordelia Donnely starts high school in a small Oregon town dominated by its Shakespeare Festival, of which her stern father is artistic director and her witty mother is a star actress. To gain independence, Portia rebels by refusing to accept a part in a play; then, to win her identity, she must confront her powerful father while not losing her two best friends.

10.27 Kirshenbaum, Binnie. **Short Subject.** Orchard Books, 1989. ISBN 0-531-05836-0.

Fourteen-year-old Audrey Alice Feldman talks and acts like a mobster from the old movies that she loves. The way Audrey figures it, some jobs have to be turned down because the odds are against you, and she sticks to small-time heists—pens and erasers and such. She worries about the day when her parents find out about her life of crime, but she knows it's bound to happen—especially when she switches to the big time.

10.28 Klass, David. **Breakaway Run.** Lodestar Books, 1987. ISBN 0-525-67190-0.

A high school student from New Jersey, Tony is living with the Maeda family in Japan. Not only does he have to cope with a new language and culture, he has to deal with feelings of isolation as an outsider. Bad news from home soon after his arrival adds to his anger and frustration, but a strong self-confidence, his love of soccer, and a developing friendship with the Maeda's daughter, Yukiko, all work together for Tony on his journey of self-discovery.

10.29 Koertge, Ron. **The Arizona Kid.** Joy Street Books, 1988. ISBN 0-316-50101-8.

Sixteen and set free for summer vacation in Arizona with his Uncle Wes, Billy is determined to fulfill some dreams. Along the way he finds that dreams must be cared for: his gay uncle, his job at the horse track, his survivalist friend Lew, and his girlfriend Cara all present problems that make dreams challenging.

10.30 Landis, J. D. **The Band Never Dances.** Harper and Row, 1989. ISBN 0-06-023721-X.

When she is thirteen, Judy Valentine's brother dies. She spends the next few years searching for stardom as the drummer in a rock band—and searching for herself as well. On her search, she meets Strobe, the leader of the band; Mark the Music, the guitarist who loves her; and Nick, the singer who can't love the women who love him. Judy's search ends on a magic night in Madison Square Garden.

10.31 Mahy, Margaret. **Memory.** Margaret K. McElderry Books, 1987. ISBN 0-689-50446-2.

After a family argument, nineteen-year-old Jonny leaves the house in search of Bonny, who had been his dead sister's best friend. Although five years have passed since his sister's death, Jonny cannot rid himself of the doubt and guilt surrounding the accident. His search for Bonny is interrupted by his finding Sophie, an elderly woman who suffers from Alzheimer's disease. In caring for Sophie, whose memory is shattered, Jonny begins to find his own way to deal with the past and think about the future.

10.32 Major, Kevin. **Dear Bruce Springsteen: A Novel.** Laurel-Leaf Books, 1987. ISBN 0-440-20410-0.

Terry Blanchard is at the end of his ninth-grade year when he begins writing letters to rock star Bruce Springsteen. He pours out all of his problems to Springsteen in these letters about his separated parents, his problems with girls, his love of music, and his trouble in school. After writing these letters for seven months, Terry makes some interesting discoveries about himself.

10.33 Mango, Karin N. **Somewhere Green.** Four Winds Press, 1987. ISBN 0-02-762270-3.

Bryony Hick is angry. Not only does she have to move from the peaceful countryside to a dilapidated old brownstone in Brooklyn, but then her parents decide to leave her and her brother and sister with a housekeeper for three months while they do anthropological research in Brazil. When the housekeeper quits after a week, the children decide to try life on their own. Bryony then learns about another side of New York with the help of her brother, sister, and Angel, the boy next door.

10.34 Matthews, Phoebe. **Switchstance.** Avon/Flare Books, 1989. ISBN 0-380-75729-X.

Life is not a sitcom for Elvy Block. First her dad takes off for California, then her mom decides New York is where her new life needs to start, and Elvy gets stuck with her cigarette-smoking, real estate–selling grandmother. Elvy feels alone and abandoned in a new neighborhood and a new school. Her life gets really complicated when her two newest friends turn out to be the school's smartest, straightest student and the biggest goof-off and prankster around. Elvy's life could turn out to be a sitcom disaster!

10.35 McFann, Jane. **Deathtrap and Dinosaur.** Avon/Flare Books, 1989. ISBN 0-380-75624-2.

Bethany Anderson's father is a career Army man, so her family has moved around a lot. By her junior year, Bethany is starting her seventeenth school. This is when she meets Starling H. Whitman V, who develops a plan to help her get even with Mr. Baldwin, their fourth-period Ancient History teacher, who picks on Bethany constantly. Their revenge involves just little things—at first.

10.36 McFann, Jane. **One More Chance.** Avon/Flare Books, 1988. ISBN 0-380-75466-5.

Cath's junior year brings "one more chance" than she bargained for. Last year's heartthrob, Tony, the pregnancy of a best friend, a father she's only seen twice in the last four years, and a boy in Spanish class—all problems that descend on Cath's very well-planned "good" junior year. The "good" year is filled with pain, anger, guilt—and a realization of her self-worth.

10.37 Miklowitz, Gloria D. **Good-Bye Tomorrow.** Laurel-Leaf Books, 1987. ISBN 0-440-20081-4.

Alex Weiss is a senior in high school. He's popular, he's on the swim team, and he has a wonderful girlfriend named Shannon Begley. Then he finds out that he has contracted AIDS-Related Complex from some blood transfusions he received the year before. As Alex faces what this means, he discovers who his true friends are.

10.38 Mullin, Penn. **The Ghosts of Black Point.** Illustrated by Damon Rarey. High Noon Books, 1989. ISBN 0-87879-653-3.

Monica Barnes quit her job on a fishing boat last summer out of fear of a storm. Now, after her junior year, she finds that no one in the village will hire a quitter. Finally hired on at the lighthouse on Black Point, she hears from the lighthouse keeper about the

Growing Up 55

ghost ships and the ghosts of the men who sailed them. This time when the storm comes, Monica is up to it, and she learns something about ghosts in the process.

10.39　Namovicz, Gene Inyart. **To Talk in Time.** Four Winds Press, 1987. ISBN 0-02-768170-X.

Twelve-year-old Luke is really happy to return to the island, where he is among friends who accept his shyness and his inability to speak under pressure. But when a neighbor's dog dies of rabies, it is up to Luke to find the mysterious young stranger who befriended the dog. In order to save a life, Luke must break through his own wall of silence.

10.40　Paulsen, Gary. **The Crossing.** Orchard Books, 1987. ISBN 0-531-05709-8.

Manny Bustos, an orphan in the streets of Juárez, dreams of crossing the bridge into the United States where he has heard that children are fed and cared for and where he can find work and live safely. In Juárez he must beg for a living. He must also spend much of his time running and hiding from the older boys who would take his few coins and from the men who would sell him into slavery and abuse. Then Manny meets Sergeant Robert S. Locke, a Vietnam veteran stationed at Fort Bliss, who comes to Juárez to drink and to block out the cries of the friends he left in Vietnam.

10.41　Pendergraft, Patricia. **Miracle at Clement's Pond.** Philomel Books, 1987. ISBN 0-399-21438-0.

When Justin, Sylvie, and Lyon find a baby while out froggin', they decide to leave it on Miss Adeline Newberry's porch, since she's the only single woman in Clement's Pond. Little do they know that the whole town will think it's a miracle baby and that Lyon will soon learn a great deal about commitment.

10.42　Pople, Maureen. **A Nugget of Gold.** Henry Holt, 1989. ISBN 0-8050-0984-1.

Sally is just a little bit of a misfit. She's a little bit too average, a little bit overweight, and more than a little bit upset over her parents' constant fighting. So she is packed off to the Australian countryside for a two-week vacation with some "sometimes" friends. There she finds mystery, friendship, and a little romance. As Sally discovers a long-lost gold nugget brooch, she also discovers herself. Interspersed with Sally's story is the bittersweet story of Ann Bird, an Australian pioneer in a rough-and-tumble gold-mining town.

10.43 Rabe, Berniece. **Rehearsal for the Bigtime.** Franklin Watts, 1988. ISBN 0-531-10504-0.

Eleven-year-old Margo is the middle child between siblings who have special talents, but the only thing people ever tell Margo is that she's cute. Just once Margo wants to be the best, so she decides to be the number-one clarinet player. She hires Misty to help her play and, with her friends, forms a group called the Unrelated Siblings. Together they're going to prove something.

10.44 Ruby, Lois. **Pig-Out Inn.** Fawcett Juniper Books, 1987. ISBN 0-449-70306-1.

Dovi Chandler's mom has taken on many different types of jobs, so when she buys the Klondike Café and Cottages in Spinner, Kansas, Dovi is prepared for another flop. The truckers, though, love Dovi's mother, and Johnny, the cantankerous cook, even comes up with some good food. Then a trucker leaves without taking his nine-year-old son with him, and Dovi discovers that a crime has been committed.

10.45 Ryan, Mary C. **Frankie's Run.** Avon/Flare Books, 1987. ISBN 0-380-70537-0.

When her best friend starts wearing makeup and chasing boys, Frankie wants none of that. She has more important things on her mind, like organizing a race for the public library. So why doesn't that cute boy with the perfect nose quit hanging around?

10.46 Ryan, Mary C. **Who Says I Can't?** Little, Brown, 1988. ISBN 0-316-76374-8.

Very simply, Tessa Talbert is a wimp. Unlike her super-confident art director mother, Tessa lives through her fantasies and avoids Rod, the hunk she has a crush on. In an impulsive decision to be popular, Tessa wins the job of high school talent show director, but she soon realizes she's made a mistake. Instead of the new life she wanted, she has nasty notes in her locker, a rebellious crew, and a mother who wants to take over for her. How, exactly, does one save face when her change of image flops?

10.47 Shyer, Marlene Fanta. **Me and Joey Pinstripe, the King of Rock.** Charles Scribner's Sons, 1988. ISBN 0-684-18941-0.

When Joey Pinstripe, a famous rock star, moves into Mary Kate's apartment building, she finds herself the center of attention at school. And when she gets the job of walking Joey's two dogs, everyone wants to know if the stories about the star are true. Then a drug dealer convinces many of the students at Mary Kate's school that Joey Pinstripe condones drugs, and a drug-use epidemic erupts. And Mary Kate feels it's all her fault.

10.48 Slepian, Jan. **Something beyond Paradise.** Philomel Books, 1987. ISBN 0-399-21425-9.

Franny Simone loves to dance, so when she gets a dance scholarship to New York, she is ecstatic. Then the realization hits that her mother needs her to stay at home with her slightly senile grandmother. She also is needed by Aled, her new boyfriend, and by her best friend, Akiko, whom she must rescue from the Institute of Instant Bliss.

10.49 Strasser, Todd. **Wildlife.** Laurel-Leaf Books, 1987. ISBN 0-440-20151-9.

Gary Specter's rock band, Coming Attractions, has just completed a ten-month world tour promoting their album "Wildlife," and the members are exhausted. Susan doesn't want to think about music for a while, Oscar wants to start his own band, and Karl can't think about anything but vodka and cocaine. Then the president of Multimedia International calls Gary into his office and persuades him to produce a new album in just a few months.

10.50 Sutton, Jane. **Definitely Not Sexy.** Little, Brown, 1988. ISBN 0-316-82325-2.

High school freshman Diane Pushkin is sick of being one of the "smart creeps"; she wants to belong to the "dumb sexies." Enter James Peterson, a gorgeous new student who goes out with college girls. Diane is determined to get his attention and gain some experience.

10.51 Walker, Mary Alexander. **Brad's Box.** Atheneum, 1988. ISBN 0-689-31426-4.

When Brad arrives from Alabama to live with Rose's family in Iowa, he has only the clothes he's wearing, a small backpack, and a mysterious wooden box with a padlock on it. He tells the family never to touch the box. Rose is intrigued by Brad but embarrassed by his presence in her high school. She has no idea what he will mean to her life.

10.52 Warner, Malcolm-Jamal, with Daniel Paisner. **Theo and Me: Growing Up Okay.** E. P. Dutton, 1988. ISBN 0-525-24694-0.

Malcolm-Jamal Warner uses letters from fans and examples from "The Cosby Show" and from his own life to illustrate teenage situations and his responses to them. Among them are friendships, family, sex, abortion, and drugs. Warner is straightforward, even risking offending his readers at times. He is also honest, admitting often that he has little to offer but his ear and his understanding. Clearly the ear is that of one who understands from experience and study. Foreword by Bill Cosby.

10.53 Wyss, Thelma Hatch. **Here at the Scenic-Vu Motel.** Harper Keypoint Books, 1988. ISBN 0-06-447001-6.

Their parents were mostly refugees from the sixties, escapees to a simpler life in Bear Flats, Idaho. And the kids became isolated from the "real" life of pick-up trucks and cruising in Pineville, until seven of them who live beyond commuting distance are sent to live in a motel, unchaperoned, in order to attend high school. Jake is a senior and the unofficial leader of a group involved in high jinks, mishaps, growing up, and learning to be proud of themselves.

11 Health

11.1 Bevan, Nicholas. **AIDS and Drugs.** Illustrated by Aziz Khan. Franklin Watts, 1988. ISBN 0-531-10625-X.

Why do addicts share needles? Could you get AIDS from a tattoo needle or from ear piercing? Is there a treatment now to cure AIDS? Answers to these and other questions about AIDS are easy to find in this well-illustrated volume. Part of the Understanding Drugs series.

11.2 Dinner, Sherry H. **Nothing to Be Ashamed Of: Growing Up with Mental Illness in Your Family.** Lothrop, Lee and Shepard Books, 1989. ISBN 0-688-08493-1.

What do you do if someone in your family is mentally ill? How should you react? How can you explain it? Psychologist Sherry H. Dinner discusses schizophrenia, eating disorders, Alzheimer's disease, and other major mental illnesses and describes ways to cope with them if they appear in your family. Index included.

11.3 Gilbert, Sara D. **Get Help: Solving the Problems in Your Life.** Morrow Junior Books, 1989. ISBN 0-688-08010-3.

This book explains how to get help for whatever problems you may have. Organizations are listed that can help you to deal with abuse, addiction, adoption, legal matters, eating disorders, suicide, and many other troubles. Other useful information is also provided, including a section that explains your rights when you seek help.

11.4 Kolodny, Nancy J. **When Food's a Foe: How to Confront and Conquer Eating Disorders.** Little, Brown, 1987. ISBN 0-316-50167-0.

Eating disorders are a major problem in the United States. A recent study of tenth-grade girls shows that 13 percent of them exhibit bulimic behavior. Another study suggests that between 1 and 4 percent of high school–aged students are anorexic. *When*

Food's a Foe offers straight facts about eating disorders, tells what you can do about them, and suggests places to get help.

11.5 Pringle, Laurence. **Living in a Risky World.** Morrow Junior Books, 1989. ISBN 0-688-04326-7.

Toxic waste, polluted air and water supplies, incurable diseases, smoking, drinking, skateboarding—life is risky. And in this book, noted science writer, Laurence Pringle explores risk and the way we've come to understand it. He asks, "How safe is safe enough?" and discusses ways to reduce the hazards of life.

11.6 Seuling, Barbara. **You Can't Sneeze with Your Eyes Open and Other Freaky Facts about the Human Body.** Illustrated by author. Lodestar Books, 1986. ISBN 0-525-67185-4.

Did you know that the distance between the inside of your elbow and your wrist is approximately the same as the length of your foot? Did you know that your brain operates on about the same amount of power that would light a ten-watt bulb? Also, by the end of each day you have shrunk almost one inch, but don't worry—you'll return to your old height by morning. These and other surprising facts about our bodies are illustrated with humorous line drawings.

12 Historical Fiction

12.1   Beatty, Patricia. **Be Ever Hopeful, Hannalee.** Morrow Junior Books, 1988. ISBN 0-688-07502-9.

The Civil War has ended. Hannalee's brother Davey, in his twenties, takes Hannalee and their family to Allanton, where Davey hopes to find work to support the family. Hannalee finds work in a store, but she is forced to hide from a Yankee soldier trying to find her. The family's troubles become "worse than war" when Davey is accused of a murder he didn't commit, and courageous Hannalee risks her life to prove his innocence. Sequel to *Turn Homeward, Hannalee*.

12.2   Conrad, Pam. **My Daniel.** Harper and Row, 1989. ISBN 0-06-021313-2.

Eighty-year-old Julia Creath visits her grandchildren and, in the special ambience of the Natural History Museum, shares with them an adventurous story of her youth in Nebraska, when she couldn't imagine anything happening to the close relationship she shared with her older brother, Daniel. Daniel's quest for dinosaur bones conflicted with the plans of a greedy paleontologist who schemed to possess the biggest dinosaur find, but he and Julia concocted a daring plan to outsmart the paleontologist.

12.3   Heuck, Sigrid. **The Hideout.** Translated by Rika Lesser. E. P. Dutton, 1988. ISBN 0-525-44343-6.

Rebecca, about nine, is found in the ruins of a bombed-out German city during World War II. Since she remembers only her first name, she is sent to an orphanage in another town. There she meets Sami, a boy who lives in a cornfield. Sami makes magic for Rebecca, taking away her hunger and fear. As the battlefront advances on the town, Rebecca's efforts to save Sami lead to a rewarding conclusion.

12.4   Matas, Carol. **Lisa's War.** Charles Scribner's Sons, 1987. ISBN 0-684-19010-9.

Share the courage, fear, and strength of Lisa, a young Jewish girl growing up in Denmark when Hitler invades in 1940. Just thirteen, she joins her brother and her best friend in the resistance movement and fights the Germans through secrecy and sabotage. Through Lisa, you'll discover the fighting spirit that helped defeat Nazi Germany and saved thousands of Danish Jews. Lisa is bright, free-spirited, and ready for the fun of being a teenager, but she discovers hardship, persecution, and bravery instead.

12.5   Nixon, Joan Lowery. **A Family Apart.** Bantam Books, 1987. ISBN 0-553-27478-3.

In this first book of a four-part series, the six Kelly children of New York City are given up for adoption by their poor, widowed mother, who hopes for a better life for them. In 1860 they are sent on the Orphan Train to St. Joseph, Missouri, where they are chosen by farm families. This first novel tells the adventures of Frances Mary, the oldest, and Petey, the youngest Kelly, as they adjust to the ways of the West.

12.6   Pearson, Gayle. **The Coming Home Cafe.** Atheneum, 1988. ISBN 0-689-31338-1.

In the summer of 1933, fifteen-year-old Elizabeth runs away from home, looking for work so she can help her family. Her father needs a job, her mother needs a doctor, her little brother needs a meal, and they all need money so the bank won't take their house. As Elizabeth rides the rails from town to town in search of a job, she discovers the Great Depression, some new friends, her fears, and her real self.

12.7   Terris, Susan. **Nell's Quilt.** Farrar, Straus and Giroux, 1987. ISBN 0-374-35504-5.

It's 1899, and Nell Edmunds wants a life that is different from her mother's: she wants to go to college. Nell's plans are crushed, however, when her parents inform her that she is to marry Anson Tanner, a widower with a young daughter. Although Nell agrees to the marriage, she gradually begins to withdraw from the world around her, obsessed with putting together scraps of material to make a quilt—an effort that may kill her.

13 History

13.1 Aaseng, Nathan. **The Rejects.** Lerner, 1989. ISBN 0-8225-0677-7.

What do Xerox, Orville Redenbacher, Birdseye, Jell-O, and Monopoly have in common? All are products or businesses that have outlived critics who said, "It will never sell." These products and inventions, as well as others, provide the basis for entertaining success stories of people who had persistence. Index included.

13.2 Anderson, Joan. **Spanish Pioneers of the Southwest.** Photographs by George Ancona. Lodestar Books, 1989. ISBN 0-525-67264-8.

Travel back in time to live with the Spanish pioneers who settled in what would become New Mexico. In pictures and story, this book follows the experiences of a boy, Miguel, recreating life as it would have been for him in the 1700s: living in an adobe fort, having run-ins with the Indians, and experiencing strong family ties and subsistence living.

13.3 Chaikin, Miriam. **A Nightmare in History: The Holocaust 1933-1945.** Clarion Books, 1987. ISBN 0-89919-461-3.

How could six million Jewish people have been systematically annihilated between 1939 and 1945? This book traces the history of anti-Semitism, then focuses on the atrocities committed against the Jewish people by the Nazis during World War II.

13.4 Duden, Jane. **1940s.** Crestwood House, 1989. ISBN 089686-475-8.

What happened in the 1940s? In 1940 Bugs Bunny made his first cartoon appearance. Pearl Harbor was bombed in 1941, and the United States entered World War II. The world's first electronic computer was used in 1946. Velcro was invented in 1948. In *1940s*, you'll find out what life in America was really like between 1940 and 1949. Part of the Timelines series. Other books in the series are *1900s*, *1910s*, *1920s*, *1930s* (by Gail Stewart), and *1950s*, *1960s*, and *1970s* (by Jane Duden). Index included.

13.5 Dudman, John. **The San Francisco Earthquake.** Illustrated by Richard Scollins. Bookwright Press, 1988. ISBN 0-531-18163-4.

Think "earthquake" and you think San Francisco. This small book presents the San Francisco Earthquake of 1906 in an easy-to-read format with many pictures, charts, and maps. There is an index, a glossary, and a list of serious earthquakes and their dates. This is a good beginning reference on the subject. Part of the Great Disasters series.

13.6 Faber, Doris, and Harold Faber. **The Birth of a Nation: The Early Years of the United States.** Charles Scribner's Sons, 1989. ISBN 0-684-19007-9.

Should the president of the United States be called His Highness? Or His Excellency? Or perhaps even His Elective Majesty? The First Congress of the United States was faced with making this decision and carrying out many other difficult tasks, as well. The important events and people of the early years of the United States are cataloged in this book—including a discussion of the Barbary Pirates and the Whiskey Rebellion.

13.7 Fisher, Dorothy Canfield. **Our Independence and the Constitution.** Landmark Books, 1987. ISBN 0-394-89175-9.

The proclamation of independence from Great Britain by the thirteen colonies was just the beginning of our new nation's difficulties. By 1787, the Articles of Confederation were failing, and a new government had to be put into place. This is the story of both the Declaration of Independence and the Constitution of the United States as seen through the eyes of the children of Philadelphia.

13.8 Fisher, Leonard Everett. **The White House.** Holiday House, 1989. ISBN 0-8234-0774-8.

The first president to live in the White House was John Adams. He and his wife, Abigail, moved in on November 1, 1800. The presidential home was originally designed by architect James Hoban during George Washington's second term. From then to George Bush's administration, the White House has had numerous changes, including the recent stripping of thirty-two layers of paint to get it ready for a new coat of gleaming white. The White House is the only residence and office of a head of state anywhere in the world that is opened to the public free of charge, even on a limited basis. Index included.

13.9 Fornatale, Pete. **The Story of Rock 'n' Roll.** William Morrow, 1987. ISBN 0-688-06276-8.

"Long live rock 'n' roll!" writes Graham Nash in this book's foreword. The story of rock music, from its beginnings to the present, is recorded in this lively history, with special emphasis on the sixties. There are dozens of photos and direct quotes from musicians. Elton John tells how he felt when he zoomed to stardom and then hit a slump. Ray Manzarek of The Doors tells us that their music had timeless messages such as coming to grips with reality, with one's own dark side, and with inner madness. The tragedy of Marvin Gaye's death is just one of hundreds of stories about the people who have made rock-and-roll history.

13.10 Lawson, Don. **The Abraham Lincoln Brigade: Americans Fighting Fascism in the Spanish Civil War.** Thomas Y. Crowell, 1989. ISBN 0-690-04697-9.

This historical account of Americans fighting in the Spanish Civil War, 1936–39, shows the international enthusiasm for democracy pitted against fascism. The book is detailed enough to vividly portray the battles and the personalities of the American leaders. The response of artists such as Hemingway and Picasso is cited, along with the heroics of American volunteers. Reading the book is a reminder of a nearly forgotten war and the struggle for democracy that predated World War II.

13.11 Meltzer, Milton. **American Politics: How It Really Works.** Illustrated by David Small. Morrow Junior Books, 1989. ISBN 0-688-07494-4.

Like it or not, politics affects every single thing in your life. This book explains how politics works in a straightforward manner. It begins with an explanation of the history of politics in the United States and finishes with both a discussion of the cost of corruption and a discussion of how individuals like you can make a difference.

13.12 Meltzer, Milton, editor. **Voices from the Civil War: A Documentary History of the Great American Conflict.** Thomas Y. Crowell, 1989. ISBN 0-690-04800-9.

After setting the stage with brief outlines of events and issues, the editor lets the words from newspapers, ballads, diaries, speeches, and letters tell the story of the Civil War. Causes of the Civil War, the war itself, and its aftermath are explored. Northern riots in protest of the draft, the loss of 38,000 black men in battle, the war at sea—all have a voice here. A bibliography and an index are included.

13.13 Perl, Lila. **The Great Ancestor Hunt: The Fun of Finding Out Who You Are.** Illustrated by Erika Weihs. Clarion Books, 1989. ISBN 0-89919-745-0.

Nearly all of us in the United States are immigrants. Whether our ancestors came by sailing ship in the 1600s or by jet just a few years ago, most of us came from somewhere else. Our ancestors may have been driven from their homelands by warfare, famine, or persecution. Tracing your family's ancestry can be fascinating, and this book tells you how to begin the quest. An index and an appendix on how to gain access to public records are included.

13.14 Russell, Alan, and Norris McWhirter, editors. **1988 Guinness Book of World Records.** Bantam Books, 1988. ISBN 0-553-27066-4.

Ashrita Furman of New York walked twenty-four miles while balancing a full pint milk bottle on his head. A boy in England was born with fourteen fingers and fifteen toes. The longest cooked noodle was 939 feet and 11 inches and was made in Colorado in 1985. This 1988 edition of the *Guinness Book of World Records* contains many amazing facts, as well as information on how you can create a world record.

13.15 Sullivan, George. **How the White House Really Works.** Lodestar Books, 1989. ISBN 0-525-67266-4.

Did you know that Richard Nixon had a bowling lane installed under a driveway leading to the White House? Did you know that in the State Dining Room no one touches a knife or fork until the president begins to eat? This book provides an insightful behind-the-scenes look at the workings of the White House.

14 How-to

14.1 Brandt, Sue R. **How to Write a Report.** Illustrated by Anne Canevari Green. Franklin Watts, 1986. ISBN 0-531-10216-5.

Report writing is a frequent assignment. This book gives step-by-step instructions for writing a report, including choosing and understanding your subject, building a bibiliography, taking notes, outlining, and writing the final draft.

14.2 Dunbar, Robert E. **How to Debate.** Franklin Watts, 1987. ISBN 0-531-10335-8.

Making your point effectively is a valuable skill. This book discusses what debating is, how to prepare for it, methods of argument, taking the affirmative stand, how the negative side attacks, listening and responding effectively, how judges make their decisions, and procedures for formal debates. A glossary of terms is included, plus debate topics and sources and a listing of annual national debate competitions. A Language Power Book.

14.3 Fowler, Virginie. **Clayworks: Colorful Crafts around the World.** Illustrated by author. Prentice Hall Books for Young Readers, 1987. ISBN 0-13-136417-0.

This book provides a history of many early clay structures from different countries. It then provides a list of necessary materials and tools as well as pictures and instructions for creating replicas of these pieces. The reader can learn how to make an Eastern Mediterranean oil lamp, an Italian fish candle holder, French interlocking tiles, an Egyptian pendant, a Chinese flowerpot, and many other clay pieces. Index included.

14.4 Murphy, Jim. **Custom Car: A Nuts-and-Bolts Guide to Creating One.** Clarion Books, 1989. ISBN 0-89919-272-6.

Watch as a burned-out Ford Fairlane, worth only about $75, is transformed into a classy custom car. What was once tame family transportation turns into a car of powerful style and powerful performance. The author and his technical consultant, Tom

Walsh, spend slightly over $5,000 and many hours in making the transformation. Includes glossary, parts list, and index.

14.5 Ryan, Margaret. **So You Have to Give a Speech!** Franklin Watts, 1987. ISBN 0-531-10337-4.

Being assigned to give a speech can produce butterflies in the stomach, but here's a book that might help ease your nerves. It covers choosing a topic, gathering information, preparing a draft, practicing, and delivering the speech. A Language Power Book.

14.6 Schmitt, Lois. **Smart Spending: A Young Consumer's Guide.** Charles Scribner's Sons, 1989. ISBN 0-684-19035-4.

Every day you are bombarded with advertisements trying to sell you something. In the face of this, *Smart Spending* discusses the best way to receive satisfaction by spending wisely to get your money's worth. The topics covered include budgeting, consumer fraud, product safety, and mail-order schemes.

15 Humor

15.1 Draper, C. G. **A Holiday Year.** Little, Brown, 1988. ISBN 0-316-19203-1.

Something always happens to Ned around holiday time. At Halloween, he's all set to do a magic show for his sister's party when an obnoxious cousin shows up and nearly ruins it all. After that, he has to decide how to deal with the live turkey his dad had given him in June, with instructions to fatten it up for the big Thanksgiving dinner. Taking care of the gobbler hasn't been easy, but killing him is not something Ned looks forward to. And so it goes. Each family holiday brings new problems and new insights.

15.2 Gilson, Jamie. **Hobie Hanson, You're Weird.** Illustrated by Elise Primavera. Lothrop, Lee and Shepard Books, 1987. ISBN 0-688-06700-X.

Hobie is depressed when his best friend, Nick, has to go away to computer camp for the summer after fourth grade. Hobie's dad wants him to have a summer like Tom Sawyer's, but Hobie's at a loss until big-mouth Molly Bosco decides she's Hobie's friend. They win a pie-eating contest together, get mentioned twice in one newspaper, and change the mayor's idea about a time capsule.

15.3 Korman, Gordon. **A Semester in the Life of a Garbage Bag.** Scholastic, 1987. ISBN 0-590-40695-7.

Raymond Jardine has never had anything but bad luck, but he's convinced that if he wins Dewitt High's summer trip to Theamelpos, Greece, his luck will change. He tricks fellow junior Sean Delancey, who has also applied for the trip, into helping him with his schemes to be sure the two are selected. Unfortunately, Raymond's schemes involve a $33 million government project and a dead poet who must come back to life for Raymond and Sean to win.

15.4 Manes, Stephen. **Chicken Trek: The Third Strange Thing That Happened to Oscar Noodleman.** Illustrated by Ron Barrett. E. P. Dutton, 1987. ISBN 0-525-44312-6.

In an attempt to win the "Bagful o' Cash" in a chicken-eating contest, Oscar Noodleman travels coast to coast in a picklemobile that belongs to his cousin, the inventor Dr. Peter Prechtwinkle. The contest gets interesting when Oscar and Peter are forced to pit their wits against an evil psychic with a grudge against Oscar's cousin. The psychic, Mrs. Gulbekian, has a huge appetite and is willing to do anything to keep Oscar from winning the contest.

15.5 Manes, Stephen. **The Great Gerbil Roundup.** Illustrated by John McKinley. Harcourt Brace Jovanovich, 1988. ISBN 0-15-232490-9.

Gerbil, Pennsylvania, was a sleepy little town until the inhabitants decided to put it on the map by building the First National Drive-Thru Museum of American Sightseeing and Clean Rest Rooms and by holding the Great Gerbil Roundup. These events fill Gerbil, Pennsylvania, with thousands of whooping tourists swinging tiny lariats, and only two kids, Elton Wazoo and McBeth McBeth, can save Gerbil from the destruction the tourists promise.

15.6 Manes, Stephen. **The Obnoxious Jerks.** Bantam Books, 1988. ISBN 0-553-05488-0.

When Frank transfers to Griswold High, he is flattered that the Obnoxious Jerks ask him to join their group. All of them are bright, hilarious, and unlike any other boys in school. The Obnoxious Jerks' specialty is "Jerk Outs," in which they challenge stupid rules, like dress codes and conformity in general. When a girl, "Iceberg" Freeze, asks to join the group, she and Frank become the focus of the all-time greatest Jerk Out, and Frank even wears a skirt to school.

15.7 Peck, Robert Newton. **Soup's Uncle.** Illustrated by Charles Robinson. Delacorte Press, 1988. ISBN 0-440-50062.

Rob and Soup are off on their tenth adventure. Soup's Uncle Virus has come to town with his motorcycle gang, the Hardboilers. The boys dream of riding Uncle Vi's motorcycle, but instead they uncover something strange in the barn next door to Janice Riker, the toughest kid in town.

15.8 Smirnoff, Yakov. **America on Six Rubles a Day; or, How to Become a Capitalist Pig.** Illustrated by Lois Lowenstein. Vintage Books, 1987. ISBN 0-394-75523-5.

In 1977, America sent millions of tons of wheat to the Soviet Union. The USSR sent us comedian Yakov Smirnoff. Upon entering the immigration office at New York's Kennedy Airport, Smirnoff asked a 400-pound woman in a green dress, "Are you the Statue of Liberty?" His perceptive and zany observations on life in the U.S. include chapters on becoming a citizen (or, "sworn in the U.S.A."), television and movies (or, "we've only just rerun"), and nice things about his homeland (or, "still crazy after all these years"). Mature subject matter.

15.9 Sobol, Donald J. **Encyclopedia Brown's Book of Wacky Cars.** Illustrated by Ted Enik. William Morrow, 1987. ISBN 0-688-06222-9.

In 1913, the Jackson Motor Company built a car with the pedals and the steering wheel in the backseat. The passengers sat in front of the driver, and the car was called the Duck. In 1910, the same company produced a car with headlights that doubled as bumpers. In this book, Encyclopedia Brown explains these and other bizarre and interesting facts from the real world of automobiles.

15.10 Tolan, Stephanie S. **The Great Skinner Getaway.** Four Winds Press, 1987. ISBN 0-02-789361-8.

The Skinners are no ordinary family. When Dad launches headfirst into his idea of the perfect summer vacation, the rest of the family thinks it might just be their ticket to adventure. At first, anyway. Their group includes Mom, Jenny, Marcia, Rick, Ben, a dog, two cats, and Brunhilda, their somewhat used thirty-five-foot motor home. Exploding appliances, a diet of wild foods, and other adventures await the zany Skinner family as they journey across America.

15.11 Trudeau, G. B. **Downtown Doonesbury.** Illustrated by author. Owl Books, 1987. ISBN 0-8050-0354-1.

Zonker goes for Dudeship, Duke returns from Haiti, and Nancy Reagan's inaugural ball gown is stretching at the rate of half an inch a year. Through his cast of comic strip characters, Trudeau takes a humorous and often stinging look at the ironies of homelessness, Nicaragua, and relations between the sexes. Mature subject matter.

16 Love and Romance

16.1 Conford, Ellen. **The Things I Did for Love.** Bantam Books, 1987. ISBN 0-553-05431-7.

When sixteen-year-old Stephanie Kasden needs a psychology project, she decides to research love. Never having been in love, she figures she could use a little more information. Stephanie sets up interviews to get some in-depth information, but then along comes Bash, the right combination of good looks and charm to give Stephanie some first-hand experience. Unfortunately, Bash is a dropout and rides a very fast motorcycle. Stephanie loses her objectivity but laughingly learns there's a lot more to love than kisses and a motorcycle ride.

16.2 Cooney, Caroline B. **Camp Girl-Meets-Boy.** Bantam Books, 1988. ISBN 0-553-27273-X.

The great advantage of being teen camp counselors for Vi and Marissa is not teaching grade-school kids, but meeting the handsome male counselors from the boys' camp nearby. But Vi and Marissa didn't expect the competition they find in stunning new dance counselor Cathy. Cathy is not merely gorgeous, she's perfect. And all the boys, including Sin and Dark, have been blinded by Cathy's beauty. They've forgotten that Vi and Marissa exist, much less that the girls have crushes on them. Is it possible that Cathy can be beaten out by ordinary girls like Vi and Marissa?

16.3 Cooney, Caroline B. **The Girl Who Invented Romance.** Bantam Books, 1988. ISBN 0-553-05473-2.

At sixteen, Kelly Williams is tired of watching everyone around her experience romance while she's not even dating anyone. When Kelly decides to invent a board game about romance, she has no idea what kinds of changes it will bring into her life and how much she'll learn about real love.

16.4 Davis, Leila. **Lover Boy.** Avon/Flare Books, 1989. ISBN 0-380-75722-2.

Love and Romance 73

It's cool to be considered the school's lover boy, until you decide you want to date a cute, smart, and really "nice" girl for a change. Then nobody trusts you, and her reputation suffers just from being near you. How do you turn off the rumor mill, get a good reputation, and convince her parents and her kid brother that you can be trusted when you aren't even sure you can trust yourself?

16.5   Elfman, Blossom. **First Love Lives Forever.** Fawcett/Juniper Books, 1987. ISBN 0-449-70155-7.

Ophelia (Phillie) has a crush on Brad and desperately wants his ring—she almost gets killed "winning" it. Phillie is super smart—she can ace honors classes and make quiche from scratch. She is also super dumb as she takes her best friend Mad Hatfield's loyalty for granted, lets the evil Eileen Cotter (who also wants Brad) copy her work in class, and underestimates her parents. She tutors Leslie Malcolm, teen model, and gains a real friend. Among Phillie's adventures, most astonishing are her "trial," her Ph.D. mom's sizzling story of her past, and the unusual ending when Leslie, Mad, and Brad converge in Phillie's bedroom, where she has decided to stay forever.

16.6   Haynes, Betsy. **The Great Boyfriend Trap.** Bantam Books, 1987. ISBN 0-553-15530-X.

Scotti Wheeler and Lorna Markham are in the seventh grade, are next-door neighbors, and are best friends. They tell each other all of their secrets except one: their secret loves. Scotti has a crush on Lorna's older brother and Lorna has one on one of their classmates, but the boys have love interests of their own. Lorna and Scotti come up with a plan that is sure to win the boys over, but they soon learn that making someone love you is a lot harder than they thought.

16.7   Kaplow, Robert. **Alessandra in Love.** J. B. Lippincott, 1989. ISBN 0-397-32281-X.

When Wyn Reed walks into the orchestra class, Alessandra takes one look and falls in love, this time for real. After all, Wyn has the *face*; besides, he's a talented musician; besides, he becomes genuinely interested in her. Just when it all seems too good to be true, Alessandra discovers a problem. She isn't the only girl in Wyn's life. Now she will have to decide what she must do to keep Wyn to herself.

16.8 Makris, Kathryn. **A Different Way.** Avon/Flare Books, 1989. ISBN 0-380-75728-1.

Steve Lansing-Ames is a Yankee who was transplanted to Texas, where everyone plays football. Steve's parents, though, won't let him play because it's so dangerous, so he's labeled a wimp. When Steve meets Addy Florio, he wants to impress her, so he joins Sam Houston High's swim team and begins to copy the guys around him. However, as Steve gets to be more of a jock, Addy pulls farther away.

16.9 Matthews, Phoebe. **The Boy on the Cover.** Avon/Flare Books, 1988. ISBN 0-380-75407-X.

Cyndi Carlisle is trying hard to locate the boy she saw on the cover of a book because she thinks he's gorgeous. She becomes obsessed with meeting him and then suddenly discovers that he goes to her school. His name is Tom Dalton, and soon he and Cyndi begin dating. Unfortunately, when Tom learns why Cyndi was attracted to him, her dreams come to an end.

16.10 Mazer, Harry. **The Girl of His Dreams.** Avon/Flare Books, 1987. ISBN 0-380-70599-0.

When he starts out on his own, eighteen-year-old Willis Pierce has dreams of someday running a race against Aaron Hill and of meeting the girl of his dreams. When Sophie Browne leaves her family farm, she wants to move to the city to become a pilot. Willis and Sophie team up to help each other realize their dreams, but it isn't until after he has lost Sophie that Willis realizes he's in love.

16.11 Pfeffer, Susan Beth. **Evvie at Sixteen.** Bantam Books, 1988. ISBN 0-553-05475-9.

Evvie Sebastian is not very happy. Her parents are forcing her to spend the summer with her nasty great-aunt, Grace, and Evvie expects it to be a nightmare. What she doesn't expect is to meet two boys who are interested in her. Evvie's aunt is not shy about voicing her opinion on the best choice, but which way will Evvie's heart tell her to go? Part of The Sebastian Sisters series.

16.12 Posner, Richard. **Goodnight, Cinderella.** M. Evans, 1989. ISBN 0-87131-587-4.

As prom night approaches, Kimber Delaney's life grows more and more complicated. Her family, her girlfriends, and her wealthy, handsome, lying boyfriend all contribute to the chaos and intrigue of what ultimately becomes "a fairy-tale romance for all young people who believe in true love and happy endings."

16.13 Santini, Rosemarie. **Beansprouts.** Fawcett Juniper Books, 1989. ISBN 0-449-70322-3.

At sixteen, Nina Norton is the only girl on the high school baseball team; she is the relief pitcher for Ron Alden. She also loves horseback riding and takes ballet lessons. Her mother keeps a tight rein on Nina, and her schedule is too full to really have fun and hang out. But Nina has a crush on Ron, and when he begins to notice her, her life changes in big ways.

16.14 Vedral, Joyce L. **The Opposite Sex Is Driving Me Crazy.** Ballantine Books, 1988. ISBN 0-345-35221-1.

Cut through the junk, the hype, and the fog. Here are the real answers boys and girls have to the questions you want to ask. Why can't guys say "I love you?" Would a guy break up with me because I refuse to have sex? Why are girls jealous? Why does a girl think I am out for only one thing? The answers come from real kids, the advice from an experienced professional.

16.15 Zable, Rona S. **Love at the Laundromat.** Bantam Books, 1988. ISBN 0-553-27225-X.

Sixteen-year-old Jo Thompson thinks her mother is crazy when she spends their savings on a run-down laundromat; but when she realizes her mother needs her help in running the business, Jo is certain her social life is ruined forever. Enter a hunk named Scott Ashley, a college student with laundry to do. Jo can't bring herself to tell Scott that she is the high school "Fluff and Fold" girl, not the fellow college student Scott thinks she is. After some wonderful dates with Scott, can Jo risk losing him by telling him the truth?

17 Mystery

17.1 Avi. **Wolf Rider: A Tale of Terror.** Collier Books, 1988. ISBN 0-02-041511-7.

When a mysterious caller threatens to kill a young woman, only Andy believes the man is for real. But Andy's friends, his father, the police, and the victim-to-be all think Andy is crying wolf. Left alone to discover the truth, Andy seeks out the stalker, only to find that the stalker now seeks him.

17.2 Bellairs, John. **The Eyes of the Killer Robot.** Bantam Books, 1986. ISBN 0-553-15552-0.

Thirteen-year-old Johnny Dixon lives with his grandparents in Massachusetts, across the street from his good friend, Professor Childermass. Together with the professor and his only other friend, Fergie, Johnny sets out to discover if the stories about a "living" robot that is activated by human eyes are true. But what neither Johnny nor his two friends realize is that the evil Evaristus Sloane, the inventor of the robot, is still alive and seeks revenge.

17.3 Bennett, Jay. **The Dark Corridor.** Franklin Watts, 1988. ISBN 0-531-15090-9.

Kerry Lanson is shocked when three teenagers in his town kill themselves, but when his girlfriend, Alicia Kent, is found dead, Kerry doubts it was suicide. As he deals with his grief, he is haunted by Alicia's father, who is blaming Kerry for Alicia's death. Then Kerry uncovers what really happened the night Alicia died.

17.4 Bennett, Jay. **The Haunted One.** Fawcett Juniper Books, 1987. ISBN 0-449-70314-2.

Even though he had saved two others while lifeguarding that summer, Paul Barrett is unable to rescue his girlfriend, Jody Miller, in time. After she drowns, Paul closes himself off from everyone. Then Jody begins calling Paul on the telephone, and he begins to see her wherever he goes. Paul knows she is dead, and yet, it is Jody he sees and Jody's voice he hears.

17.5 Branscum, Robbie. **Cameo Rose.** Illustrated by Beth Peck. Harper and Row, 1989. ISBN 0-06-020558-X.

Spirited fourteen-year-old Cameo Rose is very curious, and her curiosity gets her into trouble with her neighbors and with her grandfather, the sheriff. In the Arkansas hills, poking into everyone's business, even to help Grandpa solve a murder, is frowned upon. When someone shoots her grandfather, Cameo Rose finally gets scared and accepts help from handsome Billy Joe, but she is more determined than ever to find the murderer. Then someone shoots at her, and she must find the truth quickly.

17.6 Brown, Fern G. **Baby-Sitter on Horseback.** Fawcett Juniper Books, 1988. ISBN 0-449-70283-9.

Just fifteen minutes. That's all he was gone. Sure, it was dark and snowing. But how could a twelve-year-old boy disappear between the house and the barn in fifteen minutes? Her parents were always saying that sixteen-year-old Melissa was irresponsible—now what would they say? Then the call for ransom comes. Who could have kidnapped Scott? Melissa teams up with Daniel for two days of danger, persistence, and just plain nerve to solve the mystery of the missing boy.

17.7 Campbell, Hope. **Looking for Hamlet: A Haunting at Deeping Lake.** Macmillan, 1987. ISBN 0-02-716400-4.

Taryn Kate Powell, the daughter of actors and an actress herself, has always wanted to play Ophelia in *Hamlet*. Now, vacationing at an old manor in the Adirondack Mountains, she meets Craig. He is the grandson of the dead actress who is said to haunt the manor grounds dressed as Ophelia, and who looks just like Kate. Together, Kate and Craig decide to get to the bottom of the mystery surrounding his grandmother's drowning.

17.8 Carey, M. V. **The Case of the Savage Statue.** Illustrated by Tom Leonard. Random House, 1987. ISBN 0-394-88225-3.

In broad daylight, Jupiter, Bob, and Pete, the Three Investigators, witness a kidnapping by three foreign-looking men in turbans. The kidnappers demand the statue of the horrifying Hindu goddess Kali as ransom. The Three Investigators face decisions at every turn, and so do you. You decide what they need to do, and whether or not the mystery is solved depends upon your skills and decisions as a detective. Can you do it? A Find Your Fate Mystery.

17.9 Carey, M. V. **The Mystery of the Cranky Collector.** Random House, 1987. ISBN 0-394-89153-8.

Jupiter, Pete, and Bob, the Three Investigators, are teenagers in California who have their own private detective business. In *The Mystery of the Cranky Collector*, solving the disappearance of old Mr. Pilcher is more a question of who *wouldn't* want him out of the way than who *would*, as he is a mean man whom nobody likes. The clues to the kidnapping are few, but a cryptic message in Mr. Pilcher's computer sets the boys to investigating and wondering, who or what is Sogamoso? And who is Navarro?

17.10 Cusick, Richie Tankersley. **The Lifeguard.** Scholastic, 1988. ISBN 0-591-41549-2.

When Kelsey goes to spend the summer at the ocean with her mother's boyfriend, Eric, and his three children, she is unprepared to face the disappearance and possible drowning of Eric's daughter, Beth. Her own father drowned just two years earlier while saving Kelsey, and she still has nightmares about it. As the search for Beth continues, Kelsey begins uncovering clues that suggest that Beth was murdered, and Kelsey's knowledge makes her prey for the murderer.

17.11 Duffy, James. **Missing.** Charles Scribner's Sons, 1988. ISBN 0-684-18912-7.

Ten-year-old Kate Prescott takes a ride with a stranger in a big, black Buick and disappears. This is the suspenseful story of what happens to Kate and her sister Sandy's search for her.

17.12 Duncan, Lois. **Don't Look behind You.** Delacorte Press, 1989. ISBN 0-385-29739-4.

"You're part of the Cinemax generation. You can't believe real-life stories don't always have happy endings," is what Jim told April one night when she was complaining about being hidden in a motel room while her father testified against major drug dealers. April hates having to leave her boyfriend four days before the prom with no explanation. She doesn't understand the Witness Relocation Program, and in her efforts to retain her old life, she puts her whole family in deadly danger.

17.13 Duncan, Lois. **The Twisted Window.** Delacorte Press, 1987. ISBN 0-385-29566-9.

Tracy Lloyd doesn't understand why she allows Brad Johnson to convince her to become a part of his scheme to kidnap his half-sister back from her father. Brad claims their father stole her, and it's right for them to do this, but Tracy is scared because Brad isn't even from her town. He just showed up one day at Winfield High and introduced himself to her. Then Jamie comes to get Brad, and a scary picture unfolds before Tracy.

17.14 Dunlop, Eileen. **The House on the Hill.** Holiday House, 1987. ISBN 0-8234-0658-X.

Philip does not want to live with his great-aunt Jane, even if it is only temporary. Jane is an unsmiling woman who knows nothing about children and who lives in a gloomy old house. Philip learns, however, that both Jane and her house contain unexpected secrets. With his cousin Susan, Philip sets out to solve the mystery of the room at the top of the stairs.

17.15 Eisenberg, Lisa. **Mystery at Bluff Point Dunes.** Dial Books for Young Readers, 1988. ISBN 0-8037-0527-1.

When Kate Clancy flies off for an oceanside vacation with her high school friend Bonnie, she has no idea of the troubled party she's been invited to. Bonnie's wealthy grandparents take the girls to the family's Cape Cod cottage, where a thief stalks the halls. Kate quickly learns that the theft must be an inside job, and she pries out clues that finally put her face to face with an angry criminal. Some vacation!

17.16 Eisenberg, Lisa. **Mystery at Snowshoe Mountain Lodge.** Dial Books for Young Readers, 1987. ISBN 0-8037-0359-7.

The pranks and accidents at Snowshoe Mountain Lodge become more and more serious until Kate Clancy and her friend Bobby become convinced that someone is trying to hurt them and their classmates. Together they investigate, following a path that leads them into grave danger.

17.17 Grafton, Sue. **"F" Is for Fugitive.** Henry Holt, 1989. ISBN 0-8050-0460-2.

A confessed killer returns to Floral Beach seventeen years after the strangled body of his victim, Jean Timberlake, was found in the sand, and the case comes back to life. The killer has changed his story, and detective Kinsey Millhone agrees to help him. Kinsey plunges herself into the center of a family's emotional wound, a wound that has been festering since Jean Timberlake's death. A Kinsey Millhone Mystery. Mature language.

17.18 Hall, Lynn. **A Killing Freeze.** Morrow Junior Books, 1988. ISBN 0-688-07867-2.

Clarie likes her small hometown, she enjoys being with her father, and she is excited about the annual Winter Fest, the celebration that brings the community together and creates both interest in and money for her father's snowmobile business. This year's celebration promises to be one of the best. Then, on the morning the festivities are to begin, Clarie discovers the body of an elderly friend. When a second death occurs, Clarie discovers that her own name may be on the murderer's list.

17.19 Hall, Lynn. **Murder at the Spaniel Show.** Charles Scribner's Sons, 1988. ISBN 0-684-18961-5.

Tabby Frost works as an assistant at a first-class kennel for springer spaniels. Turner Quinn, the owner, has been blind since youth, but he has a very well-known operation, and his kennel has been chosen as the host for the national springer trials and show. His brother, Ted, has been chosen as one of the judges. Shortly after Ted arrives, he receives an anonymous death threat. Tabby, as one of Turner's assistants, is in an excellent position to watch all the trainers, handlers, owners, and judges. She is also in an excellent position to find herself next on the hit list.

17.20 Hildick, E. W. **The Ghost Squad and the Prowling Hermits.** E. P. Dutton, 1987. ISBN 0-525-44330-4.

The members of the Ghost Squad are determined to keep the evil Dr. Purcell from succeeding in his plan to have his ghostly accomplices take over the temporarily vacated bodies of living beings. Book 5 in the Ghost Squad series.

17.21 Holland, Isabelle. **Thief.** Fawcett Juniper Books, 1989. ISBN 0-449-70269-3.

Cressida has no memory of what happened to her between the time her parents were killed and when she ended up living with her hateful Aunt Romaine and cousin Alison. After she's accused of stealing, she ends up living with her half-brother Alaric and his wife, Brenda. Ten years later, events begin repeating themselves, and Cressida is in danger of being institutionalized for stealing.

Mystery

She knows that the secret of what is happening lies buried in what she can't remember.

17.22 Holland, Isabelle. **The Unfrightened Dark.** Little, Brown, 1990. ISBN 0-316-37173-4.

Suddenly, Jocelyn, blind since she was twelve, is the target of something hostile and threatening. Voices of strangers—and one in particular—accuse her of making a slave of her guide dog, Brace. Other people's pets disappear mysteriously. Finally, when her beloved Brace vanishes, Jocelyn and her friends decide that it is time to act.

17.23 Howard, Elizabeth. **Mystery of the Deadly Diamond.** Illustrated by Michael William Kaluta. Random House/Byron Preiss Books, 1987. ISBN 0-394-87549-4.

Living in Paris in 1900, Paris MacKenzie, the daughter of a French-born father and an American mother, becomes involved with murder and deceit and an evil woman named Meduse. Paris and her friend Violette explore the floor of the Seine River in an experimental diving bell and find a trunk that may be linked to the theft of a priceless diamond. Part of the My Name Is Paris series.

17.24 Howard, Elizabeth. **Mystery of the Magician.** Illustrated by Michael William Kaluta. Random House/Byron Preiss Books, 1987. ISBN 0-394-97547-2.

Paris MacKenzie, a young American, came to France to visit her uncle, who, unfortunately, was found dead the day she arrived. She is further surprised to learn that she has inherited his house, but that does mean that she can stay a while longer. She does not realize, however, that she will become involved in the theft of a valuable mirror and the abduction of the famous magician, Harry Houdini. Part of the My Name is Paris series.

17.25 Howard, Elizabeth. **Mystery of the Metro.** Illustrated by Michael William Kaluta. Random House/Byron Preiss Books, 1987. ISBN 0-394-87546-X.

In 1900, Paris MacKenzie, a Chicago teenager, is invited by her uncle to spend a year in France. She is wildly excited about the prospect. Her parents are pleased, too: her father, being French, wants Paris to learn something about his country. When she arrives, however, she discovers that her uncle is dead, presumably of a heart attack. Paris doesn't believe his death was from natural causes and, in the best tradition of her hero, Sherlock Holmes, she determines to solve the mystery. Part of the My Name Is Paris series.

17.26 Howard, Elizabeth. **A Scent of Murder.** Illustrated by Michael William Kaluta. Random House/Byron Preiss Books, 1987. ISBN 0-394-87548-6.

Living in Paris at the turn of the century, Paris MacKenzie and her friend Marcel Fleury have been invited to visit the famous painter Claude Monet. Shortly after their arrival, Paris discovers a body among the lily pads. Of course, many assume that the death was an accident, but Paris believes it was murder. Once more, Paris is determined to solve the crime. Part of the My Name Is Paris series.

17.27 Hurwitz, Johanna. **The Cold and Hot Winter.** Illustrated by Carolyn Ewing. Morrow Junior Books, 1988. ISBN 0-688-07839-7.

When Bolivia returns to Woodside, New Jersey, to visit her relatives for Christmas vacation, her friends Derek and Rory are ecstatic. Then Bolivia's Swiss army knife disappears, followed by Derek's hamster and nineteen dollars from Derek's special safe. Unfortunately, Rory is the prime suspect. Derek doesn't know what to do. How do you accuse your best friend of being a criminal? Sequel to *The Hot and Cold Summer*.

17.28 Jaspersohn, William. **Grounded.** Bantam Books, 1988. ISBN 0-553-05450-3.

When you're grounded and expelled and not meeting anyone's expectations (even your own), maybe you need some time to get away. That's what sixteen-year-old Joe Flowers decides as he hitchhikes to Cape Cod. The girl he meets there, Nan Wright, helps him to hide, and he helps her to figure out the mysterious happenings on her rich grandfather's island. Joe and Nan get to know each other, and they learn about themselves while they become deeply involved in a deadly plot that may be too big for them to handle.

17.29 Johnston, Norma. **Return to Morocco.** Four Winds Press, 1988. ISBN 0-02-747712-6.

It's a long way from a Texas debut to a Mediterranean cruise, but a cruise is exactly what seventeen-year-old Tori Clay wants. She gladly leaves the world of social butterflies behind, but when she and her grandmother arrive in Morocco, she glimpses some dark secrets about her grandmother's experiences there during World War II. With the help of a handsome new friend, who might become more than a friend, Tori learns the truth about her grandmother—and about herself.

17.30 Kidd, Ronald. **Second Fiddle: A Sizzle and Splat Mystery.** Lodestar Books, 1988. ISBN 0-525-67252-4.

A practical joker has invaded the Pirelli Youth Orchestra. Now the overhead sprinklers go on during Handel's *Water Music*; the bass drum demands better treatment of instruments; and during *Finlandia*, the tuba player find his instrument packed with *fish*! But when fireworks cause a fire that destroys a valuable violin, the two young sleuths, Sizzle and Splat, realize that the situation is serious and the time for solving the mystery is running out.

17.31 Miller, W. Wesley. **Blain's Woods.** Illustrated by Jack Lucey. High Noon Books, 1988. ISBN 0-87879-618-5.

When Peter and Pam Hanson move out to the country, they are very excited about building their first tree house. However, as they work on it, strange things begin to happen. First, they feel as if they are being watched, and next someone dismantles their tree house. Then they begin to hear strange stories about events that occurred in the woods in the past.

17.32 Murrow, Liza Ketchum. **Fire in the Heart.** Holiday House, 1989. ISBN 0-8234-0750-0.

Molly O'Connor wishes someone, just anyone, would talk about her mother, who died in a car crash ten years ago. When the subject comes up, Molly's father gets angry, her brother withdraws, and her grandmother just looks sad. Then when Molly accidentally reads a letter to her father that mentions her mother, she starts off on her own search for the truth. Her reluctant grandmother, her understanding stepmother, and crazy Aunt Sadie help Molly put the pieces together in an adventure story that leads her to the gold country of California.

17.33 Nelson, Ginger K. **The Pirate's Revenge.** Illustrated by Damon Rarey. High Noon Books, 1989. ISBN 0-87879-654-1.

Janet dreamed that she met a pirate ancestor. She woke up with a stone and a key, but she didn't remember that the old pirate had given them to her in a secret room. Then, while Janet, her brother

Steve, and his friend Rob are home alone during a storm, a tree struck by lightning seems to grow around the house. The three are frightened by strange noises, a black bird, and images on the TV until finally Janet finds the answer to what's going on.

17.34 Nixon, Joan Lowery. **The Dark and Deadly Pool.** Laurel-Leaf Books, 1987. ISBN 0-440-20348-1.

Sixteen-year-old Mary Elizabeth Rafferty has always felt too tall and too clumsy. Her secret dream is to direct a symphony, but the dream she shares with her parents is to find a tall boyfriend. Mary Elizabeth is enjoying her summer job in the Ridley Hotel's exclusive health club when she becomes involved with a murder. As Fran, a coworker, tries to help her unravel the mystery, they grow close. The only problem is that he's four inches shorter than she is.

17.35 Nixon, Joan Lowery. **The Island of Dangerous Dreams.** Laurel-Leaf Books, 1989. ISBN 0-440-20258-2.

Andrea's parents are having marriage problems, so Andrea is sent to spend a month with her Aunt Madelyn, who resembles the wicked queen in Disney's *Snow White*. Andrea's aunt takes her to Judge Arlington-Hughes's island in the Bahamas for a weekend auction of an ancient Peruvian artifact. Her aunt wants to buy it for the museum where she is curator, but some other people on the island want it, too—some badly enough to murder.

17.36 Pike, Christopher. **Last Act.** Archway Paperbacks, 1988. ISBN 0-671-64980-9.

When Melanie wins the starring role in the school play, she gains the acceptance that she's longed for at her new high school. However, things turn sour on opening night when someone puts real bullets in the gun that Melanie fires during the last act.

17.37 Shaw, Diana. **Lessons in Fear.** Joy Street Books, 1987. ISBN 0-316-78341-2.

The most-hated teacher at Thomas A. Dooley High School has begun to have accidents. First she slips and knocks herself unconscious. Next she's almost electrocuted. Then she's trapped in an elevator. The accidents are getting more serious each time, and fifteen-year-old Carter Colburn is convinced that they're not really accidents. Carter works to find the culprit—and eventually finds herself up against the "Ambassadors of Doom." A Carter Colburn Mystery.

17.38 Shreve, Susan. **Lucy Forever and Miss Rosetree, Shrinks.** Henry Holt, 1987. ISBN 0-8050-0340-1.

Together, sixth-grader Lucy Childs and her best friend, Rosie Treeman, pretend to be psychiatrists in Lucy's basement. Then, they meet Cinder, a real little girl being treated by Lucy's psychiatrist father. Cinder doesn't talk because of an experience that frightened her very much. When Lucy and Rosie, playing at psychiatry, help Cinder to talk, all of their lives are placed in danger.

17.39 Shusterman, Neal. **The Shadow Club.** Little, Brown, 1988. ISBN 0-316-77540-1.

Jared and Cheryl are sick of being second best and they know others who feel the same way, so they form the Shadow Club to get some innocent revenge on those students at the top. Soon, however, a little innocent fun turns into dangerous pranks. The question is, who is behind these pranks? Is it a member of the club, or someone who is trying to frame them?

17.40 Snyder, Zilpha Keatley. **Janie's Private Eyes.** Delacorte Press, 1989. ISBN 0-440-50123-7.

The Stanley family is a mixed-up group of brothers and sisters and stepbrothers and stepsisters and stepmothers and stepfathers and geniuses and crazy kids and just plain kids. When the neighborhood dogs start disappearing, Janie (the brains of the family) is determined to find out the who, where, and why of the mystery, especially when people begin to suspect a friendly Vietnamese family who has just moved into town.

17.41 Wallace, Bill. **Danger in Quicksand Swamp.** Holiday House, 1989. ISBN 0-8234-0786-1.

The Louisiana summer holds a lot of surprises for Ben and Jake, but they don't know it yet. They think mowing lawns will be the only way to get the boat they want, until the unusually dry spring turns up a sunken boat. When they discover a treasure map under the seat, their curiosity gets the better of them, and they are off to search the dangerous Quicksand Swamp. Alligators, poisonous snakes and quicksand are nothing compared to the murderer they have to face there. Ben and Jake will need all the courage, skill, and guts they have to make it through Quicksand Swamp.

18 Poetry

18.1 Fleischman, Paul. **I Am Phoenix: Poems for Two Voices.** Illustrated by Ken Nutt. Harper and Row, 1985. ISBN 0-06-021881-9.

From the noisy, squabbling sparrow to the "common" egret, from the lonely albatross to the immortal phoenix, these poems and the accompanying illustrations celebrate the sights and sounds of birds. Meant to be read by two voices (or by two groups of voices), the poems capitalize on rhythm and imagery to bring the birds dramatically to life.

18.2 Glenn, Mel. **Class Dismissed II: More High School Poems.** Photographs by Michael J. Bernstein. Clarion Books, 1986. ISBN 0-89919-443-5.

The times have changed, but the concerns remain the same. Students, joined by a few graduates in this new edition, continue to be concerned about sports, success, sex, religion, and threats to world peace; and they continue to reflect honesty, hope, joy, cynicism, and despair. Their stories are universal.

18.3 Janeczko, Paul B. **Brickyard Summer.** Illustrated by Ken Rush. Orchard Books, 1989. ISBN 0-531-05846-8.

With the ending of school comes the bonfire—spelling lists, spiral notebooks, all the reminders of the year just completed go up in smoke. The narrator wanders through the summer thinking about high school. He becomes acquainted with all kinds of people in his hometown and discovers courage, vitality, and surprises. In reminiscing about his best friend, he learns that his strength is friendship.

18.4 Janeczko, Paul B., compiler. **Going Over to Your Place: Poems for Each Other.** Bradbury Press, 1987. ISBN 0-02-747670-7.

This collection of 132 poems reflects impressions of everyday love and loss by such poets as Adrienne Rich, May Swenson, John Ciardi, and Stanley Kunitz. Topics range from the opening poem by Peter Meinke, "The Heart's Location," to a first kiss, to arm wrestling, to shooting crows, to a belly dancer, to the final poem by Ted Kooser, "At Midnight."

18.5 Knudson, R. R., and May Swenson. **American Sports Poems.** Orchard Books, 1988. ISBN 0-531-05753-4.

America believes in sporting events and in sports heroes. The poem may be about Jackie Robinson or Casey's daughter with the enthusiastic crowds; it may concern the player who says, "What I like best/Is shooting baskets by myself." Some may want to go "out to the ball game"; others may be "Watching Football on TV." Whatever the subject of the individual poem, this collection is firmly rooted in the American sports tradition.

18.6 Koch, Kenneth, and Kate Farrell, editors. **Talking to the Sun: An Illustrated Anthology of Poems for Young People.** Metropolitan Museum of Art and Henry Holt, 1985. ISBN 0-87099-436-0.

The poems in this collection represent the past and the present and speak of many different cultures. Poems vary in subject and style—from the nonsensical to the serious, from sonnets to haiku. All of the illustrations are reproductions from the collections of the Metropolitan Museum of Art.

18.7 Komunyakaa, Yusef. **Dien Cai Dau.** Wesleyan University Press, 1988. ISBN 0-8195-1164-1.

What was it like to be in Vietnam, to wait, camouflaged, in ambush, to smell the stench of disease and excrement and death, to know that many comrades will not survive, to realize that going home may not bring release? Through these poems, Komunyakaa mirrors the anguish that war creates.

18.8 Wagoner, David. **Through the Forest: New and Selected Poems, 1977–1987.** Atlantic Monthly Press, 1987. ISBN 0-87113-153-6.

"To be successful/And serene we must be at one with the universe." Wagoner's poetry reflects his thesis as he celebrates the flight of the hungry hawk and the loss of the snapping turtle. He writes of his father, the workman, the wage earner; and of his mother, the selfless giver. Greek mythology, childhood and young adulthood, fact and fantasy—all are part of this celebration of life and of human experience.

19 Science

19.1 Berger, Melvin. **The Science of Music.** Illustrated by Yvonne Buchanan. Thomas Y. Crowell, 1988. ISBN 0-690-04645-6.

If you want to know the how and why of music, this book is for you. How does a voice sing? How do instruments make their unique sounds? How do you make sense of the musical language? How do you make a record, and how does a record make music when it's played? What is sound, anyway? This book lets you understand, practice, and build your own music.

19.2 Bleifeld, Maurice. **Experimenting with a Microscope.** Illustrated by Anne Canevari Green. Franklin Watts, 1988. ISBN 0-531-10580-6.

This book covers the history of the microscope, how to use a microscope, and what to look for when viewing everything from salt to bread mold to pond water to razor blades. A list of scientific supply companies, a list of books for further reading, and an index are also included for those curious about exploring the world around them.

19.3 Branley, Franklyn M. **Mysteries of Life on Earth and Beyond.** Illustrated by Sally J. Bensusen. Lodestar Books, 1987. ISBN 0-525-67195-1.

"For hundreds of years, many people believed there were Moon people. In fact, in 1835, a newspaper printed a story describing the Moon people as having wings like those of a bat." In this book, distinguished astronomer Franklyn Branley discusses the significant research that has been done concerning the existence of intelligent life on other planets in our galaxy. Part of the Mysteries of the Universe series.

19.4 Chaple, Glenn F., Jr. **Exploring with a Telescope.** Illustrated by Anne Canevari Green. Franklin Watts, 1988. ISBN 0-531-10581-4.

An explanation of telescope types, parts, care, and accessories is included in the opening chapters. The book then gives instruction for viewing land, the moon, the sun, the stars, and other deep-space objects. Magazines and books to read, sources of equipment, astronomical organizations, and an index are included.

19.5 Cobb, Vicki. **Why Doesn't the Earth Fall Up? And Other Not Such Dumb Questions about Motion.** Illustrated by Ted Enik. Lodestar Books, 1988. ISBN 0-525-67253-2.

Science comes from asking questions, and this book makes it fun to ask—and answer—those questions. Illustrations help you understand the rolling, swinging, spinning, falling, world of science. Try your hand at some experiments, and start asking questions and solving scientific puzzles of your own.

19.6 Crofford, Emily. **The Great Auk.** Crestwood House, 1989. ISBN 0-89686-459-6.

A survivor of the Ice Ages, the great auk, a relative of the puffin, finally became extinct about a hundred years ago after centuries of being hunted for its feathers and as a source of food. In 1835, naturalists believed that only about fifty great auks were left. Museums were alarmed that future generations would not be able to see what the great auk looked like and sent crews out to bring back specimens to stuff. They brought back forty-eight. Includes addresses to write for more information, a glossary, and an index. Part of the Gone Forever series.

19.7 Duggleby, John. **The Sabertooth Cat.** Crestwood House, 1989. ISBN 0-89686-462-6.

Imagine a 500-pound lion with 9-inch fangs—that's the sabertooth cat of 12,000 years ago. Instead of biting its prey, the big cat drove its fangs home for the kill. This big cat roamed North America for thousands of years and disappeared with the Ice Age. Over 2,000 skulls of the sabertooth have been recovered from the La Brea tar pits in Los Angeles. Includes glossary, index, and address to write to for more information. Part of the Gone Forever series.

19.8 Dunnahoo, Terry. **The Lost Parrots of America.** Crestwood House, 1989. ISBN 0-89686-461-8.

Several species of parrots are now extinct, among them, the Carolina parakeet, believed to be the only member of the parrot family native to the United States. In addition, many species of parrots are now on the endangered list. The parrots' popularity as a pet, the destruction of the South American rain forests, and the use of bird feathers as decoration are dangers facing the parrot family. Includes glossary, index, and address to write to for more information. Part of the Gone Forever series.

19.9 Harrar, George, and Linda Harrar. **Signs of the Apes, Songs of the Whales: Adventures in Human-Animal Communication.** Simon and Schuster Books for Young Readers, 1989. ISBN 0-671-67748-9.

Animal language experiments over the last twenty years have proven that at least some animals are more than just "dumb" creatures. For instance, Koko, a gorilla has learned over five hundred signs and has even invented a number of signs of her own, including abstract ones for "above" and "below." Experiments with dolphins and whales often focus on the use of sound rather than signs and have proven that these animals recognize the significance of word order. These experiments have given science new insights into animal intelligence. Index included. A *Nova* book.

19.10 Horn, Gabriel. **Steller's Sea Cow.** Crestwood House, 1989. ISBN 0-89686-460-X.

A type of manatee, the Steller's sea cow lived for thousands of years near the Bering Strait. Believed by some to be mermaids, the manatee females gave birth to live young and nursed them much as other mammals do. The Steller's sea cow was also unique in that it lived in cold water; other manatees require warm. Within twenty-seven years of its discovery in the 1700s, the Steller's sea cow was extinct. Part of the Gone Forever series.

19.11 Isberg, Emily. **Peak Performance: Sports, Science, and the Body in Action.** Simon and Schuster Books for Young Readers, 1989. ISBN 0-671-67750-0.

The modern technology used in sports training centers today has helped athletes of all kinds to perform at their peak. Technology has also helped design the most effective sports equipment used for maximum performance and prevention of injury. Sports medicine and the technology behind it make significant contributions to the well-being of athletes in all arenas, but this book focuses on Olympic athletes and the work of the U.S. Olympic Training Centers. Index included. A *Nova* book.

Science

19.12 Kettelkamp, Larry. **Computer Graphics: How It Works, What It Does.** Morrow Junior Books, 1989. ISBN 0-688-07504-5.

Today animation, mapmaking, and video games all depend on computer graphics, a combination of technology and art. Computer graphics have dramatically changed the ways in which illustrations can be drawn and expanded the ways in which illustrations can be used. This book explains the how and why of the many applications of computer graphics.

19.13 Lee, Sally. **Donor Banks: Saving Lives with Organ and Tissue Transplants.** Franklin Watts, 1988. ISBN 0-531-10475-3.

Did you know that skin and bones, as well as eyes and blood, can be saved and transplanted? Sally Lee tells of case after case of organ and tissue transplants that have saved or improved lives. The problems, research, and processes involved in maintaining organ banks and in donating organs are carefully detailed. The book also contains a glossary, index, and list of further resources. The author concludes with information on how to become an organ or tissue donor.

19.14 Math, Irwin. **Wires and Watts: Understanding and Using Electricity.** Aladdin Books, 1989. ISBN 0-689-71298-7.

Did you ever make a battery out of a lemon? This book teaches the basics of electricity and magnetism through experiments and projects that produce actual working models. The projects use common, inexpensive materials.

19.15 Maurer, Richard. **Junk in Space.** Simon and Schuster Books for Young Readers, 1989. ISBN 0-671-67768-3.

A space census indicated that, as of September 30, 1988, 7,122 objects were orbiting the earth. Of those objects, 1,734 were payloads, of which only 350 were still working. On top of that, the first moon exploration and the five later landings left behind a total of twenty tons of "junk." What is this junk? What hazards does it create? This book explores answers to those questions. A *Nova* book.

19.16 Mell, Jan. **The Atlantic Gray Whale.** Crestwood House, 1989. ISBN 0-89686-458-8.

By studying fossils and sailors' journals, scientists have patched together the story of the Atlantic gray whale and its extinction.

Fossils have been found in Europe and, between 1850 and 1979, ten fossils were found off the eastern shore of the United States. Other species of gray whales are currently at risk of extinction. Perhaps regulating whaling and recognizing present-day dangers to gray whales will help save them. Includes glossary, index, and addresses to write to for more information. Part of the Gone Forever series.

19.17 Morrison, Susan Dudley. **The Passenger Pigeon.** Crestwood House, 1989. ISBN 0-89686-457-X.

September 1, 1914, marked the death of Martha, the last passenger pigeon in the world. At one time, passenger pigeons numbered in the millions and flew in flocks large enough to block out the sun. As the eastern part of the United States became more crowded, the passenger pigeons moved farther west. The pigeons were easy to kill, and hunters pursued them for sport, for food, and for their feathers, which were used to decorate hats. By the time people became concerned about the pigeons' fate and passed laws to protect them, it was too late. Includes glossary, index, and addresses to write to for more information. Part of the Gone Forever series.

19.18 Pearce, Q. L. **Quicksand and Other Earthly Wonders.** Illustrated by Mary Ann Fraser. Julian Messner, 1989. ISBN 0-671-68530-9.

We live on perhaps the most amazing planet in our solar system. Astonishing facts about our planet are introduced and illustrated here—moving continents, the Great Rift Valley, the Arctic tundra, the La Brea tar pits, and many more. The mysteries of the saguaro cactus, ant farmers, and spider silk are also explored. Includes bibliography and index. Part of the Amazing Science series.

19.19 Sanford, William R., and Carl R. Green. **The Dodo.** Crestwood House, 1989. ISBN 0-89686-455-3.

Before it became extinct, the dodo was found on three islands off the coast of Africa. Although it is classified in the same family as the pigeon, the dodo was a much larger, flightless bird, which was believed to have weighed around fifty pounds. The last dodo was seen about three hundred years ago. Its disappearance marked the first recorded extinction of an entire species. Includes address to write to for more information, glossary, and index. Part of the Gone Forever series.

Science

19.20 Sanford, William R., and Carl R. Green. **The Woolly Mammoth.** Crestwood House, 1989. ISBN 0-89686-456-1.

The woolly mammoth stood taller than any elephant alive today and must have been a fearful sight to prehistoric peoples. Its coat of shaggy fur made the mammoth appear even larger. The first bones of this ancient giant were found over five hundred years ago, and since that time, more discoveries have led to various theories about the woolly mammoth, its life, and, finally, its extinction. Includes address to write to for more information, glossary, and index. Part of the Gone Forever series.

19.21 Symes, R. F. **Rocks and Minerals.** Photographs by Colin Keates and Andreas Einsiedel. Alfred A. Knopf, 1988. ISBN 0-394-89621-1.

Beautiful photographs of rocks and minerals make this volume a good resource for readers who want to identify rocks. This book also contains photos of gemstones; some information on cutting, polishing, and collecting rocks and minerals; and even information on rocks from space. An Eyewitness Book.

20 Science Fiction

20.1 Asch, Frank. **Journey to Terezor.** Holiday House, 1989. ISBN 0-8234-0751-9.

Matt Hilton and his parents are kidnapped by aliens and taken to a galactic preserve for endangered species. In the Earth colony there, Matt meets Ryan and Sara, two young geniuses with plans to escape the preserve and return to Earth. As their adventure develops, Matt is forced to impersonate an alien from another colony of the preserve, and Sara and Ryan are "despaced"—converted into miniature black holes by the spherical robots that both imprison and serve the colonists. Part 1 of the Orb Trilogy.

20.2 Blackwood, Gary L. **The Dying Sun.** Atheneum, 1989. ISBN 0-689-31482-5.

Ahead of an ice age that has moved steadily southward, most North Americans have gone south, to stop finally in northern Mexico. James and his family are among the travelers; but now, in 2050, conditions in Mexico are rapidly getting worse. James's family decides to return north. Although they know they will face primitive conditions and isolation if they go north, they prefer that to the terrorist activities of the fanatics who call themselves the Mexican Liberation Army. James initially decides to stay in Mexico; however, as destruction worsens, James begins the long journey to rejoin his family.

20.3 Blair, Cynthia. **Freedom to Dream.** Fawcett Juniper Books, 1987. ISBN 0-449-70263-4.

Katy Norris hates history. She can't figure out why everyone is making such a big deal about the bicentennial anniversary of the U.S. Constitution. One day, however, a freak accident sends her back to 1787, and she has the opportunity to experience the big event for herself.

20.4 Brooks, Bruce. **No Kidding.** Harper and Row, 1989. ISBN 0-06-020722-1.

In the middle of the twenty-first century, the human race has solved numerous problems. War and disease are pretty much a thing of the past. Children are generally authority figures. Sam, age fourteen, makes the decisions in his family about his mother's being institutionalized for acute alcoholism, his brother's schooling, and his brother's adoption. Sam discovers that, although he's very bright and very caring, he cannot always have complete control and that his carefully made plans for his family's survival may go astray.

20.5 Caraker, Mary. **The Snows of Jaspre.** Houghton Mifflin, 1989. ISBN 0-395-48292-5.

In the twenty-fourth century, Morgan Farraday is assigned to a job on the planet Jaspre, an Earth colony. Sent to Lumisland in the north, she is drawn to the colored snows, and there she meets Anders Ahlwen, a mystic who has the powers of the snow. When Morgan's daughter, Dee, joins Ahlwen's camp, her father tries to rescue her and, in the attempt, comes to accept Ahlwen's power. Morgan then finds a way to perhaps save the snows from progress.

20.6 Christopher, John. **When the Tripods Came.** E. P. Dutton, 1988. ISBN 0-525-44397-5.

On what had promised to be a routine orienteering expedition, fourteen-year-old Laurie and his friend Andy witness the first invasion of the Tripods. When that invasion is apparently repulsed, people relax, only to be invaded by a second attack far more subtle than the first. When Laurie and his family recognize that the Tripods intend to brainwash everyone with hypnotic caps, they desperately try to flee the country. Part of the Tripods series.

20.7 Gilden, Mel. **Harry Newberry and the Raiders of the Red Drink.** Henry Holt, 1989. ISBN 0-8050-0698-2.

It sounds crazy, but Harry Newberry believes his own mother is the comic book superhero Tuatara. Can Harry, Tuatara, and a loony gang of misfit superheroes stop the dreaded Bonnie Android from destroying Yupitz and turning it into a supergalactical work of art? Other questions this book will answer: Can smelly gym socks destroy your brother? Can anchovies ever be loved? Can cheese blight cure the common cold? Can cold, day-old pizza be a commercial success? After this adventure, ordinary comic books will never be the same!

20.8 Hoobler, Thomas. **Dr. Chill's Project.** G. P. Putnam's Sons, 1987. ISBN 0-399-21480-1.

At age fifteen, Allie is released from a home for the mentally ill into the custody of Dr. Chill, who runs a home where he experiments with his residents' psychic abilities. He pushes Allie to develop her special talent, which she then uses to rescue a friend whom Dr. Chill has allowed the government to kidnap.

20.9 Mullin, Penn. **Message from Outer Space.** Illustrated by Michael Cincotta. High Noon Books, 1988. ISBN 0-87879-616-9.

When Don's employer at Computer Town, Mr. Jenkins, disappears from his wheelchair, there is a strange message left on the computer screen. It explains that Mr. Jenkins had to be taken because he knew too much about another world. With the help of his friend, Leroy, Don tries to find Mr. J. before it's too late.

20.10 Pfeffer, Susan Beth. **Rewind to Yesterday.** Illustrated by Andrew Glass. Delacorte Press, 1988. ISBN 0-440-50048-6.

Kelly Forrest hates school. She wants to be an explorer; what does school have to do with that? Soon Kelly is to learn that life is more interesting than she could have imagined. Kelly's father brings home a VCR and life is changed forever when she discovers the magic that the machine holds within it. Will she be able to use the machine for the good of humanity?

20.11 Riding, Julia. **Space Traders Unlimited.** Atheneum, 1988. ISBN 0-689-31409-4.

Streak is a Portkid in a Martian city who barely exists by scrounging and trading for food and for air for his air tank. After an explosion in the middle of a trade fair, Streak finds himself involved in a series of events that involve him with the head executives of the big corporation, Space Traders Unlimited, to whom Streak feels he owes a debt. Attempting to repay his debt, Streak becomes involved in bombings and sabotage and has to face a past that he has tried hard to forget.

20.12 Service, Pamela F. **A Question of Destiny.** Collier Books, 1988. ISBN 0-02-044981-X.

Dan Stratton's father is running for president. One day Dan discovers that his father's chief adviser, David Greer, is not who he seems. Greer has a calculator that uses unusual symbols, and his childhood neighbors don't remember him. To help his father, Dan must find out who Greer really is, where he comes from, and what he's up to.

20.13 Spremich, Andrew. **Flight of the Dragon.** Illustrated by Jack Lucey. High Noon Books, 1988. ISBN 0-87879-619-3.

Eric, Professor Chang, and Burt the robot leave Earth aboard the Dragon in order to go to the planet Trant. Eric is hoping to locate the Azak spaceship that crashed earlier and discover the mind-reading machine. Eric doesn't know, though, that there are others looking for the machine, too, and that he and his friends will be involved in more than one rescue attempt.

21 Social Problems

21.1 Becerra de Jenkins, Lyll. **The Honorable Prison.** Lodestar Books, 1988. ISBN 0-525-67238-9.

Marta Maldonado's father is an outspoken journalist. When he refuses to stop criticizing his country's dictator, he and his family are removed from their home and imprisoned in a house in the Andes. Marta, her parents, and her brother must learn to survive in a totally new environment.

21.2 Berger, Gilda. **USA for Africa: Rock Aid in the Eighties.** Franklin Watts, 1987. ISBN 0-531-10299-8.

Rock music has become a vehicle for reaching out to those in need. British musicians, with their Band Aid effort in 1984, and a group of over forty-five American stars who sang "We Are the World" in 1985 helped generate funds for famine relief programs in Africa. Live Aid, Farm Aid, and the album *Sun City* were additional outreach efforts to confront the issues of hunger, the struggling American farmer, and apartheid in South Africa.

21.3 Childress, Alice. **Those Other People.** G. P. Putnam's Sons, 1989. ISBN 0-399-21510-7.

Jonathan Barnett, at seventeen, is a temporary computer instructor at Minitown High School. Not only does his age seem to work against him, but one of the students—a popular, older teacher who is being forced by the administration to take Jonathan's class—is determined to make Jonathan look bad. When the older teacher attempts to rape a student, the only witnesses are a black student—one of two in the school—and Jonathan, who has some secrets of his own. The school board holds a hearing, and Jonathan determines to tell the truth, regardless of the cost.

21.4 Collier, James Lincoln. **The Winchesters.** Macmillan, 1988. ISBN 0-02-722831-2.

Fourteen-year-old Chris was born a Winchester but not raised as one. Therefore, he cannot understand why his friends and their

Social Problems

families are turning against him when labor unrest occurs at the Winchester factory, where most of the townspeople work. Chris's cousin, Ernest, who goes away to school, is being groomed to eventually take over the business. However, Chris goes to the public school and has grown up with the local children. Now, Chris must decide on which side his loyalties lie.

21.5 Crutcher, Chris. **Chinese Handcuffs.** Greenwillow Books, 1989. ISBN 0-688-08345-5.

Dillon Hemingway and his brother Preston are often mistaken for twins even though Preston is two years older. Then Preston loses his legs in a motorcycle accident, and the boys' lives change dramatically. When Dillon is forced to watch Preston commit suicide, his own life becomes a shambles. With the help of his brother's girlfriend, and with his friend Jennifer Lawless, Dillon begins to try to put his life back together. Then he discovers that Jen has the most terrible secret of all.

21.6 Fine, Anne. **My War with Goggle-eyes.** Joy Street Books, 1989. ISBN 0-316-28314-2.

At Kitty Killin's girls school in Scotland, a pained outburst from a schoolmate triggers Kitty's sharing of how she, too, coped with her divorced mother's boyfriend, whom she nicknames Goggle-eyes. To get rid of this middle-aged political idiot, Kitty sabotages him at every chance. But her mother and sister continue to be devoted to him, and he continues to show patience in the face of her open dislike. Then an unexpected event prompts a change in Kitty's viewpoint about his place in their family.

21.7 Forman, James D. **Cry Havoc.** Charles Scribner's Sons, 1988. ISBN 0-684-18838-4.

A toddler is torn to pieces, apparently by the family poodle. The dog is destroyed. Then a young cheerleader turns up missing, and when her body is discovered, she, too, has been mutilated and torn almost beyond recognition. The quiet little town of Sandy Cliffs is terrorized by what seems to be a wild animal, but what in fact may be the result of a top-secret government research project in which genetic manipulation has changed ordinary dogs into programmed killers.

21.8 Hamilton, Virginia. **A White Romance.** Philomel Books, 1987. ISBN 0-399-21213-2.

Black runner Talley Barbour never planned to become friends with Didi, one of the white students being bused to Colonel Glenn High School. Longing for a different life, Talley is entranced with Didi's "white romance" with heavy metal rocker Roady, and she is attracted to Roady's friend David. But drugs threaten both "white romances," and Talley must weigh her survival against her exotic romance.

21.9 Harris, Mark Jonathan. **Come the Morning.** Bradbury Press, 1989. ISBN 0-02-742750-1.

Ben's father, Clyde, disappeared from the family's El Paso home, but Ben is certain that his father has gone to Los Angeles to get a new start and that when he gets situated, he will send for his family. When a money order arrives from LA, Ben believes that Clyde is inviting them to join him, and the family heads for Los Angeles. For Ben, though, the City of Angels turns out to be the city of broken dreams.

21.10 Holbrook, Sabra. **Fighting Back: The Struggle for Gay Rights.** Lodestar Books, 1987. ISBN 0-525-67187-0.

Approximately 10 percent of all people are gay, and again and again, this portion of our population is denied basic human rights because of their sexual orientation. This book is about the rights denied them and about how they are trying to beat the prejudice and ignorance that causes the denial.

21.11 Malmgren, Dallin. **The Ninth Issue.** Delacorte Press, 1989. ISBN 0-385-29691-6.

When Blue Hocker enters his new high school in Texas, he realizes that the gymnasium alone is bigger than his former high school. But the comparisons don't end there. A top athlete in his former school, Blue doesn't have a chance in the new one. Exasperated, he quits the team and joins the high school newspaper staff. The staff and the sponsor are determined to have a quality paper, although some of their stories are firmly opposed by the administration. When a Supreme Court ruling changes the rules and the sponsor's job is in danger, the controversy explodes.

21.12 Miklowitz, Gloria D. **Secrets Not Meant to Be Kept.** Laurel-Leaf Books, 1987. ISBN 0-440-20334-1.

Adri is certain there is something very wrong with her. She really likes her boyfriend, Ryan, but every time he touches her, she pulls away. When her three-year-old sister, Becky, begins having nightmares, Adri is pushed into remembering the experiences she had at Treehouse Preschool as a child. Becky is going there now, and Adri is terrified that Becky is facing what she did.

21.13   Morris, Winifred. **Dancer in the Mirror.** Fawcett Juniper Books, 1987. ISBN 0-449-70285-5.

Carole thinks that Marty's friendship is almost too good to be true. Before Marty, Carole's life was a depressing maze of trying to avoid her parents' divorce, her mother's drug habit, and her father's womanizing habit. Marty is beautiful and sophisticated, and Carole is more than happy to let her take the lead, especially with boys. Marty becomes the dancer, and Carole is the mirror. But when Marty leads Carole into a dangerous dance called death, Carole must make a decision.

21.14   Morton, Jane. **No Place for Cal.** Avon/Camelot Books, 1989. ISBN 0-380-75548-3.

Twelve-year-old Cal has been shuttled from foster home to foster home, and he has run away from every one he's been placed in. At night, Cal has dreams about being hungry and lonely, and he wants to live with his mother. Then one day at school, the social worker accidentally tells him where his mother lives, and Cal's journey begins.

21.15   Peck, Robert Newton. **Arly.** Walker, 1989. ISBN 0-8027-6856-3.

It is 1927, and Arly Poole and his father live among the pickers in Jailtown, Florida. Poor and illiterate, the pickers are ruled by boots, whips, and beatings. When a schoolteacher comes to town, Arly's father is determined that Arly will have a chance to read and write. Arly wants to learn, and the teacher sees him as a very promising young man. The people in power, however, see only that education for anyone is not in their own best interests.

21.16   Samuels, Gertrude. **Yours, Brett.** Lodestar Books, 1988. ISBN 0-525-67255-9.

When she is four, Brett Jarrett's parents get divorced. A neighbor's complaint about her mother's inadequate care sends Brett to a foster home, the first in a ten-year series of foster homes, where she begins to build up resentment against her father and resentment for being a throwaway kid. Finally, a caring caseworker,

Brownie, offers Brett a chance for the stable family she never had. Can someone as bitter as Brett fit into a normal family again?

21.17 Seixas, Judith S. **Living with a Parent Who Takes Drugs.** Greenwillow Books, 1989. ISBN 0-688-08627-6.

Case studies help illustrate the problems families face when drug abuse is a part of their lives. Each case study is followed by a discussion of the problems, as well as possible solutions. The summary explains the classifications and effects of various drugs.

21.18 Strasser, Todd. **The Accident.** Delacorte Press, 1988. ISBN 0-440-50061-3.

After four of his good friends are killed in a drunk driving accident, Matt Thompson tries to find out what happened that night. The only survivor won't talk, and it takes the police a week to decide on the accident's cause. Then Matt receives a letter in the mail that confirms his suspicions, and he begins uncovering facts that someone has gone to great lengths to hide.

21.19 Swindells, Robert. **A Serpent's Tooth.** Holiday House, 1989. ISBN 0-8234-0743-8.

Lucy's family has just moved to Yorkshire, a bad move as far as Lucy is concerned. Tension increases because Lucy's father wants to protect his new job and her mother wants to promote a cause—protecting the village from becoming a nuclear waste disposal site. When the community learns that the proposed site also served as a burial ground for Black Plague victims in 1349, Lucy discovers that times may change, but people don't.

21.20 Tapp, Kathy Kennedy. **The Sacred Circle of the Hula Hoop.** Margaret K. McElderry Books, 1989. ISBN 0-689-50461-6.

As Robin trudges toward the hospital to see her sister Jen, she relives the months during which she and her family have recognized Jen's strange behavior, her significant personality changes, and finally her attempted suicide. Robin wants to unravel the mystery behind these changes so that Jen can recover and the family can be whole again.

21.21 Wersba, Barbara. **Wonderful Me.** Harper and Row, 1989. ISBN 0-06-026361-X.

Sixteen-year-old Heidi Rosenbloom is astonished by the arrival of anonymous, flowery love letters during her summer vacation.

Then she decides not to attend college after graduation the following year. When Heidi's father angrily cuts off her allowance to teach her about the real world, she finds a well-paying summer job exercising dogs in New York's Central Park. The writer of the love letters is surprisingly revealed, forcing Heidi to make a difficult decision about the appropriateness of her suitor. Mature readers.

21.22 Wolff, Virginia Euwer. **Probably Still Nick Swansen.** Henry Holt, 1988. ISBN 0-8050-0701-6.

For Nick Swansen, Room 19 is a barrier and a haven. As a Special Ed kid, he knows he's different from the other students, but he's not sure why. His friend Shana has just "gone up" to regular classes, and Nick doesn't understand what that means either. While he might not learn some things as fast as other students, Nick does have the same emotional struggles and questions. How do you ask a girl to the prom? What do you do when she accepts? How do you deal with rejection? And in the end, how do you find acceptance for the person you are? Nick takes chances, loses, and wins.

22 Sports

22.1 Anderson, Dave. **The Story of Basketball.** William Morrow, 1988. ISBN 0-688-06748-4.

Considered to be the purest of American sports, developed by Americans for Americans, basketball originated nearly a hundred years ago in 1891. Developed by James Naismith, the game originally had thirteen rules, some of which remain unchanged today. During the century of its existence, basketball has become one of the world's most popular sports because of its simplicity—all that is needed is a ball and a hoop, and it can be played by a team of two to five people or simply by yourself. Foreword by Julius Erving.

22.2 Boehm, David A., and others. **1989–90 Guinness Sports Record Book.** Sterling, 1989. ISBN 0-8069-6711-0.

This book gives not only various kinds of records for many games and sports, it also outlines short histories of many sports. Did you know that the earliest baseball game played under the Cartwright rules was in 1846 and that the youngest major league player started his career at the age of fifteen? Did you know that the longest Monopoly game lasted for 660 hours? Fascinating facts abound in sports and games from aerobatics to yachting.

22.3 Coombs, Charles. **Soaring: Where Hawks and Eagles Fly.** Photographs by author. Henry Holt, 1988. ISBN 0-8050-0496-3.

From a student pilot's first lesson in gliding through the first solo to a cross-country flight, you can learn firsthand about the sport of gliding. This book contains information on how to get a student certificate and has many photographs, a glossary, and other related resources.

22.4 Crutcher, Chris. **The Crazy Horse Electric Game.** Laurel-Leaf Books, 1987. ISBN 0-440-20094-6.

Willie is his hometown's hero. He's a super athlete, a pretty good kid, and a minor legend when he leads the home team to victory in the Crazy Horse Electric baseball game. Those are the days when Willie believes his body is his friend, that he can make no demands that his body can't meet. The world is his. Then comes the waterskiing accident, and Willie is brain damaged, his speech is altered, and his physical coordination is destroyed. The world is no longer his, but he fights to hang on to the good things.

22.5 Deuker, Carl. **On the Devil's Court.** Joy Street Books, 1988. ISBN 0-316-18147-1.

Seventeen-year-old Joe Faust is facing his last year of high school, and he wants to spend it in the public high school close to his home. His father, a renowned scientist, has other ideas and wants Joe to attend an exclusive private school. At first, Joe gets his choice, but a mistake in judgment lands him in the private school. A basketball star, he tries to make the team in his new school but doesn't do very well until one day, while he is practicing in an abandoned gym, he finds himself in an unusual situation and makes a bargain that he will ultimately regret.

22.6 Dygard, Thomas J. **Forward Pass.** Morrow Junior Books, 1989. ISBN 0-688-07961-X.

Because Frank Gardner has a reputation as a winning coach, he has been brought in to lead the Aldridge High Panthers to a victorious season. The community has not had a conference championship in nearly a dozen years, and they want one. The problem lies in the team's not having a really good pass receiver. The coach discovers a solution when he realizes that one of the basketball players is a natural. It's an unusual solution, though, because the basketball player is a girl.

22.7 Harris, Jonathan. **Drugged Athletes: The Crisis in American Sports.** Four Winds Press, 1987. ISBN 0-02-742740-4.

The statistics are staggering, but this book helps make them personal. This book looks at who takes drugs, from the pros to the amateurs, and why. The reasons range from muscle building to stress to pressure to succeed. Jonathan Harris talks about the effects drugs have on the player and on sports in general. He also discusses treatment and prevention of drug abuse.

22.8 Klass, David. **Wrestling with Honor.** Lodestar Books, 1989. ISBN 0-525-67268-0.

When the county demands that all athletes be tested for drugs, Ron Woods, wrestler and star student, goes ahead with the test even though he believes his rights are being violated. When the test comes back positive, the entire community is shocked, because Ron is the straightest kid in school. Friends, teachers, coaches—all try to get him to retake the test, but Ron refuses. His moral stand creates problems for him, yet he stands firm. His mother defends him, but Ron strongly misses the support of his father who died in Vietnam, and his bitterness about his father's absence makes his decision even harder.

22.9 Knudson, R. R. **Rinehart Shouts.** Farrar, Straus and Giroux, 1987. ISBN 0-374-36296-3.

Shy Arthur Rinehart dreads a summer without his athletic best friend, Zan, and he's determined to spot as many birds as he can that are the blue of Zan's baseball bat. Determined that Arthur will see the birds on his hope list, Arthur's millionaire grandmother purchases a racing shell and pays her absent-minded chauffeur, Hal Slappy, to help Arthur spot birds near her Potomac River home. As Arthur confronts his fear of the water, Hal and Grandmother become obsessed with the idea of actually *racing* the shell, the *Read More*, in the President's Cup Regatta. Twelfth in a series of books about Zan and Arthur.

22.10 Marek, Margot. **Matt's Crusade.** Four Winds Press, 1988. ISBN 0-02-762271-1.

Matt Tyson comes from a football family and a football town. However, after he makes the middle school team, Matt becomes involved with the local nuclear protest movement. When they invite him to participate in a demonstration, Matt must decide whether to risk it all—football, family trouble, even arrest—for the sake of the cause.

22.11 Miklowitz, Gloria D. **Anything to Win.** Delacorte Press, 1989. ISBN 0-385-29750-5.

Cam Potter is a powerful quarterback and captain of the football team. His coach believes that he has a strong possibility of getting a college scholarship—if he can gain thirty pounds in the next few months. The coach suggests that Cam take steroids and sends him to a supplier. Cam begins to gain weight, but other parts of his life deteriorate. When he realizes that his supplier, also a user, has developed cancer of the liver, Cam recognizes that he alone must make the critical decisions about his own life.

22.12 Scott, Elaine. **Choices.** Morrow Junior Books, 1989. ISBN 0-688-07230-5.

When students from Woodrow High steal the Millington High cougar, the traditional tomato/green pepper war is left behind, and the football rivalry between the two schools turns ugly. Beth O'Connor, a minor offender, is arrested and forced into a battle that could destroy her senior year.

22.13 Sullivan, George. **Big League Spring Training.** Henry Holt, 1989. ISBN 0-8050-0838-1.

To the superstars, spring training is like spring break, "a time for back slaps and wisecracks." For other players, spring training is serious business. In this book, sportswriter George Sullivan provides expert insight into the ritual that all of the players must survive in order to play in the big leagues.

23 Supernatural

23.1 Aiken, Joan. **Give Yourself a Fright: Thirteen Tales of the Supernatural.** Delacorte Press, 1989. ISBN 0-440-50120-2.

Whirl yourself away to England for thirteen quick visits with the strange and supernatural. The stories are about very real people. The bad guys are cruel, vengeful, or just plain mean. Their victims are mostly kids who win in the end. The supernatural elements include ghosts and muses, a Chinese duck, a strange owl, curses, and insanity. While these stories are definitely strange, a touch of English humor makes many of them rather fun.

23.2 Bedard, Michael. **A Darker Magic.** Avon/Flare Books, 1989. ISBN 0-380-70611-3.

Miss Potts remembers too well the dark magic of Professor Mephisto's performance at the Caledon depot fifty years before. She also remembers Freddie's death, and her feeling that it was somehow connected to his volunteering to go on stage during the magic show. Now, fifty years later, the handbill announcing the professor's magic show has reappeared, and it's up to her to save this new generation from his black magic.

23.3 Conford, Ellen. **Genie with the Light Blue Hair.** Bantam Books, 1989. ISBN 0-553-05806-1.

Jeannie Warren, a practical, smart, just-turned-fifteen year old, is just crazy enough to make a wish when a genie pops out of her birthday-present lamp. But this genie is a little out of practice, and Jeannie gets her wishes in wild, crazy, and out-of-this-century ways. Love from an "older man"? Poof! He becomes her father! The surprises never stop in this light-hearted look at the teenager who can have it all . . . if only she can ask for it in the right way.

23.4 Cunningham, Marilyn. **A Place of Power.** Illustrated by Damon Rarey. High Noon Books, 1989. ISBN 0-87879-651-7.

Tammy Jensen, fifteen, is thrilled that she can finally accompany her father on a logging trip. However, she has a frightening experience when they are at the site. Did the old man who warned the loggers to leave have special powers? Did the trees move around, and did Tammy ride a Kelpie? Not sure of anything when it's over, Tammy is left wondering about "places of power."

23.5 Douglas, Marjie. **Matrix Witch.** Gemstone Books, 1988. ISBN 0-87518-356-5.

Meaghan Lake is not a typical junior in high school; she is a white witch. With her mother's help, she is learning to handle her powers so that she can take on the even bigger powers of the Matrix, her inheritance from her father. Then she meets Mal and immediately falls in love, but her attention is pulled away by Gemma, an evil black witch who challenges Meaghan's powers.

23.6 Dunlop, Eileen. **The Valley of Deer.** Holiday House, 1989. ISBN 0-8234-0766-7.

Anne Farrar and her family have rented a house in an ordinary, boring valley. Life seems normal until Anne discovers an old family Bible which contains the name Alice Jardyne and the phrase, "deid the 24 juin 1726 blottit owt of the Boke of Lyffe." Anne determines to find out why anyone would be subjected to such a cruel fate. When she learns that Alice was believed to be a witch and was murdered, she also discovers the cost of that knowledge.

23.7 Gabhart, Ann. **Wish Come True.** Avon/Flare Books, 1988. ISBN 0-380-75653-6.

Alyssa has always made wishes, but when she finds the old mirror in Aunt Reva's attic, her wishes start coming true. Then Aunt Reva starts warning her about the mirror. It had been her sister's mirror, and there are strange stories surrounding her sister's death. When Alyssa realizes the power of the mirror, her need for it is already too strong.

23.8 Gates, Susan. **The Burnhope Wheel.** Holiday House, 1989. ISBN 0-8234-0765-5.

Ellen is bored and unhappy. She and her mother argue most of the time, and she believes that her father is a loser. One day she sees an old bus—with an unusual driver—headed for Burnhope, a community that has no bus service. Intrigued but frightened, Ellen boards the bus, telling herself that she is in control and that she can stop the adventure when she chooses. The bus driver,

23.9 Hall, Lynn. **Dagmar Schultz and the Powers of Darkness.** Charles Scribner's Sons, 1989. ISBN 0-684-19037-0.

Dagmar Schultz has a terrific crush on James Mann, but he barely acknowledges her existence. Then one night in the local bowling alley, Dagmar meets Edgar, who claims to be a warlock and offers her a deal. If she will get Edgar a date with her Aunt Gretchen, he will use his powers to capture James for Dagmar. Although she is skeptical, Dagmar agrees. Desperate situations call for desperate measures.

23.10 Hildick, E. W. **The Ghost Squad and the Menace of the Malevs.** E. P. Dutton, 1988. ISBN 0-525-44439-4.

In this adventure, the Ghost Squad encounters Clem Jackson, a mild, unassuming man on the outside but an enraged paranoid killer on the inside. The Ghost Squad's efforts to stop Jackson from causing more "accidental" deaths are complicated by the appearance of an old enemy who returns as a super ghost, capable of entering other ghostly bodies. It is up to the Ghost Squad to prevent the spread of this supernatural menace. Part of the Ghost Squad series.

23.11 McGraw, Eloise. **The Trouble with Jacob.** Margaret K. McElderry Books, 1988. ISBN 0-689-50447-0.

Jacob is a riddle. When he meets Andy Peterson, Jacob urgently tells Andy, "Someone's got my bed." Then he disappears into the woods. After other odd incidents with Jacob, Andy and his twin sister Kat decide to explore the riddle—a riddle that can only be solved in a graveyard.

23.12 Miller, W. Wesley. **The Dark Secret.** Illustrated by Jack Lucey. High Noon Books, 1988. ISBN 0-87879-620-7.

As soon as Jim sets up a clubhouse on the second floor of the old house, his personality begins to change. First, Jim becomes very attached to a picture of an old man, and he won't let anyone remove it from the wall where he found it. Then his friends begin to notice that at times he talks like an old man, and an eerie secret begins to unfold.

23.13 Pageler, Elaine. **Runaway Magic.** Illustrated by Damon Rarey. High Noon Books, 1989. ISBN 0-87879-652-5.

Lance has always wanted to be a magician, but he needs new tricks to impress his young friends. When he is asked to help Duncan the

Great move his magic show for the school assembly, Lance sees his chance to learn some new magic. But when Duncan's evil marionette tries to end Lance's dream, Lance and Joe must search for a way to end the threat of runaway magic.

23.14 Peck, Richard. **Voices after Midnight.** Delacorte Press, 1989. ISBN 0-385-29779-3.

Chad is quite uneasy about the New York City townhouse that his family has rented. Although the house is very modern and extremely comfortable, Chad knows that the voices he hears after midnight do not exist only in his imagination. When he learns that his little brother Luke hears them too, the boys investigate and begin to slip in and out of their own time.

23.15 Radford, Ken. **The Cellar.** Holiday House, 1989. ISBN 0-8234-0744-6.

Toughened and made wise by a series of foster parents, Siân is not an ordinary girl. When two elderly sisters hire Siân as a companion at their boardinghouse, "Cradle of the Winds," Siân is pleased and excited at the prospect of a more predictable life. The boardinghouse has a life of its own, though: winds whisper, and a faraway child sings lullabies. Then Siân finds the old diary of lonely Sarah Jane and reads tales of being locked in the cellar and seeing a devil. Realizing how alike she and Sarah are, Siân dares to go beyond a secret door to the cellar.

23.16 Silverstein, Herma. **Mad, Mad Monday.** Lodestar Books, 1987. ISBN 0-525-67239-7.

Did you ever wonder what would happen if you goofed when you mixed up a love potion? It's March 19, the night of dreams, and Miranda Taylor is about to find out. The result of her goof is *M*ichael *O*liver *N*ewberry or *MON*day to his friends. Monday was a seventeen-year-old "really hip dude" who died in 1958. Now he wants revenge on his old girlfriend and can't quite get the hang of the 1980s. Miranda agrees to help him, and the funny escapades that follow will keep you laughing. In the end, Miranda discovers the real secret ingredient in love potions.

23.17 Van Oosting, James. **Maxie's Ghost.** Farrar, Straus and Giroux, 1987. ISBN 0-374-34873-1.

It's Halloween, and Maxie hates wearing a costume. Every Halloween the director of the orphanage where he lives talks him into dressing up as a ghost. Maxie complains that only first graders wear sheets. However, when Maxie gets struck by lightning and meets a special ghost of his own, things change.

23.18 Whitehead, Victoria. **Chimney Witch Chase.** Illustrated by Linda Fay North. Orchard Books, 1988. ISBN 0-531-05772-0.

All Ellen wants is to run in the Midsummer Sports Meet. But her witch friends, who just happen to live in her bedroom's old chimney, want Ellen to do much more—all in fun, of course. What a mess they make! And what a wacky effort it takes to undo the mischief and get Ellen in the race.

23.19 Wright, Betty Ren. **A Ghost in the Window.** Holiday House, 1987. ISBN 0-8234-0661-X.

The only good thing about the summer, according to Meg Korshak, is the terrific acting role she grabbed in the local summer theater. Maybe she'll be too busy to worry about her parents' break-up or about her sick grandmother. Her summer plans shatter, though, when she finds herself reluctantly staying with her father in a small lakeside village because her mother "needs to get away." Once Meg is there, she discovers the mystery of a bank robbery and the ghost of Caleb Larsen's father, who tries to talk to Meg through her dreams. Sequel to *A Secret Window*.

23.20 Wrightson, Patricia. **Balyet.** Margaret K. McElderry Books, 1989. ISBN 0-689-50468-3.

When Mrs. Willet goes to tend the sacred sites of her people, the Australian aborigines, Jo sees no harm in tagging along. Her mother is gone, and she has stayed with Mrs. Willet before. What Jo doesn't know—and what Mrs. Willet had almost forgotten—is that Balyet, a young aboriginal girl who had been banished by her people a thousand years ago, still roams the hills, desperate for companionship and love. These forces, combined with Jo's rebelliousness, lead the two women—one young, one old—on a dangerous journey.

24 Travel

24.1   Armitage, Ronda. **New Zealand.** Photographs by Chris Fairclough. Illustrated by Stefan Chabluk. Bookwright Press, 1988. ISBN 0-531-18158-8.

You will want to visit New Zealand when you discover this reference book for your history, geography, or culture report. The photographs are large and beautiful, and the book is easy to read and clearly organized. Like other books in the Countries of the World series, this one contains a wealth of up-to-date information. The author is a New Zealander and a former teacher.

24.2   Beatty, John. **Earthborn: In Celebration of Wild Places.** Sierra Club Books, 1989. ISBN 0-87156-684-2.

If all the world has been explored, is there any adventure left for you? Climb the Scottish Highlands, descend into the Grand Canyon, cling to the ragged coast of Ireland, ski the icecaps of Greenland. In photographs and story, John Beatty shows what it means to seek out wild places.

24.3   Corning, Josie. **Denver, Colorado.** Crestwood House, 1989. ISBN 0-89686-464-2.

Nestled at the base of the spectacular Rocky Mountains, Denver, the Mile High City, is an exciting center of culture, professional sports, education, and recreation. Visitors have access to museums, parks, theaters, and recreation facilities, as well as quick access to many fine ski resorts in winter and summer recreation sites. Includes statistics, addresses to write for more information, a map, and an index of people and places. Part of the See the USA series.

24.4   Deegan, Paul J. **Nashville, Tennessee.** Crestwood House, 1989. ISBN 0-89686-468-5.

Nashville is perhaps best known for its country music. The Grand Ole Opry, a famous radio show, drew many performers to the city, and from that a large music industry developed. Opryland, a theme park, provides rides, adventures, and live musical productions. Visitors may also see showboats; record their own hit song; or visit parks, museums, or the world's only exact-size replica of the Parthenon. Includes statistics, addresses to write to for more information, a map, and an index of people and places. Part of the See the USA series.

24.5 Deegan, Paul J. **New York, New York.** Crestwood House, 1989. ISBN 0-89686-467-7.

New York City is situated at the mouth of the Hudson River and has one of the best natural harbors in the world. That alone makes it one of the world's best-known cities. Fondly called the "Big Apple," New York City can provide the visitor with outstanding theaters, museums, sports events, and tours of the United Nations, the Statue of Liberty, the Empire State Building, and many historic sites. Includes statistics, a map, addresses to write to for more information, and an index of people and places. Part of the See the USA series.

24.6 Einhorn, Barbara. **West Germany.** Photographs by Chris Fairclough. Illustrated by Malcolm Walker. Bookwright Press, 1988. ISBN 0-531-18187-1.

Your report on West Germany will be easy and fun if you use this book by Barbara Einhorn. Clear maps, colorful photographs, and lots of interesting details make this a very useful reference for research in geography, history, or culture for middle school and junior high. Part of the Countries of the World series.

24.7 Gregory, Lee. **Los Angeles, California.** Crestwood House, 1989. ISBN 0-89686-466-9.

Los Angeles is the second largest city by population in our country and the largest in area. Boasting everything from ocean and beaches to mountains close by, La Brea tar pits to Hollywood, Disneyland to whale watching, Los Angeles is truly a visitor's paradise. Includes statistics, addresses to write to for more information, a map, and an index of people and places. Part of the See the USA series.

24.8 Nielsen, Nancy J. **Boundary Waters Canoe Area, Minnesota.** Crestwood House, 1989. ISBN 0-89686-465-0.

A beautiful 200-mile stretch of wilderness in northern Minnesota provides a special place for those who seek solitude and natural beauty. Each year, many visitors come to the Boundary Waters Canoe Area to enjoy canoeing, camping, hiking, fishing, swimming, snowshoeing, and skiing, as well as cooking over campfires, watching sunsets, and looking for plants and animals to photograph or draw. All without radios, fast food, motorboats, or comfortable beds! The book includes clothing and equipment lists, area statistics, a map, addresses to write to for more information, and an index. Part of the See the USA series.

24.9 Sproule, Anna. **Great Britain.** Photographs by Chris Fairclough. Illustrated by Stefan Chabluk. Bookwright Press, 1988. ISBN 0-531-18157-X.

Do you think you know everything about Great Britain because you know that the British drive on the "wrong" side of the road and that America was once a British colony? This small book will make you think again. With a wealth of fascinating, up-to-date detail presented in a clear, colorful format, this is an excellent reference. You will like the photography, the large, clear maps and charts, and the glossary and index at the end of the book. Part of the Countries of the World series.

24.10 Stephenson, Sallie. **Orlando, Florida.** Crestwood House, 1989. ISBN 0-89686-463-4.

One of the world's most popular tourist attractions, Walt Disney World, is found in Orlando. More than ten million people visit Disney World each year. However, Orlando has more to offer. The NASA launch complex and the Kennedy Space Center are nearby, and St. Augustine, Daytona Beach, and many other interesting places are within easy driving distance. Includes statistics, addresses to write to for more information, a map, and an index of people and places. Part of the See the USA series.

24.11 Taitz, Emily, and Sondra Henry. **Israel: A Sacred Land.** Dillon Press, 1987. ISBN 0-87518-364-6.

Your report on Israel can start with this well-researched, easy-to-read, colorful book on that fascinating Middle Eastern country. The authors are American, but they have visited Israel more than twenty times, and their love of the country is evident. Sondra Henry and Emily Taitz write especially for young people and include many photos of young Israelis throughout the book. They also include a glossary, an index, and a list of Israeli consulates in the United States to help the reader who wants even more information. Part of the Discovering Our Heritage series.

24.12 Turck, May. **Chicago, Illinois.** Crestwood House, 1989. ISBN 0-89686-469-3.

A hard-working industrial city, Chicago was officially organized in 1831. By 1871, the year of the Great Chicago Fire, the village of 200 had grown to 300,000 people. Today it is a city of three million people that provides visitors with many interesting places to explore. Among these are the Museum of Science and Industry, the Adler Planetarium, the Sears Tower, the Lincoln Park Zoo, and the Shedd Aquarium. Includes statistics, addresses to write to for more information, a map, and an index of people and places. Part of the See the USA series.

24.13 Turck, Mary. **Washington, D.C.** Crestwood House, 1989. ISBN 0-89686-470-7.

Our nation's capital city has many points of interest, and walking tours are but one way of seeing some of them. Tourmobiles provide transportation for those who prefer not to walk. This book gives hints for enjoying Washington, including the Smithsonian, the memorials, and museums for kids. The book also includes a brief history of the city, statistics, addresses to write to for more information, a map, and an index of people and places. Part of the See the USA series.

24.14 Young, Donald, with Cynthia Overbeck Bix. **The Sierra Club Book of Our National Parks.** Little, Brown and Sierra Club Books, 1990. ISBN 0-316-97744-6.

From the great beauty of the Grand Canyon and the Rocky Mountains to the spectacular volcanoes of Hawaii, Washington, and Alaska; from lakes and forests to unusual cliff dwellings, the U.S. National Parks not only preserve many natural wonders but also give visitors a chance to participate in educational and recreational activities. The history of the National Park system is examined and the changes happening today which threaten the future of our national parks are discussed. Includes a map; a list of the U.S. National Parks with areas, features, and activities; and an index.

Directory of Publishers

Aladdin Books. Imprint of Macmillan Publishing Company. Orders to: Riverside Distribution Center, Front and Brown Streets, Riverside, NJ 08075.

Arcade Publishing. A subsidiary of Little, Brown and Company. Orders to: 141 Fifth Avenue, New York, NY 10010.

Archway Paperbacks. Division of Simon and Schuster, 1230 Avenue of the Americas, New York, NY 10020.

Atheneum. Imprint of Macmillan Publishing Company. Orders to: Riverside Distribution Center, Front and Brown Streets, Riverside, NJ 08075.

Atlantic Monthly Press. Distributed by Little, Brown and Company. Orders to: 200 West Street, Waltham, MA 02154.

Avon Books. Orders to: P.O. Box 767, Dresden, TN 38225.

Ballantine Books. Division of Random House. Orders to: 400 Hahn Road, Westminster, MD 21157.

Bantam Books. Division of Bantam Doubleday Dell Publishing Group, 666 Fifth Avenue, New York, NY 10103.

Bookwright Press. Distributed by Franklin Watts. Orders to: P.O. Box 1726, Danbury, CT 06816.

Bradbury Press. Distributed by Macmillan Publishing Company. Orders to: Riverside Distribution Center, Front and Brown Streets, Riverside, NJ 08075.

British American Publishing. Distributed by Simon and Schuster, 1230 Avenue of the Americas, New York, NY 10020.

Clarion Books. Distributed by Houghton Mifflin. Orders to: Wayside Road, Burlington, MA 01803.

Collier Books. Imprint of Macmillan Publishing Company. Orders to: Riverside Distribution Center, Front and Brown Streets, Riverside, NJ 08075.

Commonwealth Press, P.O. Box 3547, Radford, VA 24143.

Crestwood House. Distributed by Macmillan Publishing Company. Orders to: Riverside Distribution Center, Front and Brown Streets, Riverside, NJ 08075.

Thomas Y. Crowell. Distributed by Harper and Row. Orders to: Keystone Industrial Park, Scranton, PA 18512.

Delacorte Press. Division of Bantam Doubleday Dell Publishing Group, 666 Fifth Avenue, New York, NY 10103.

Michael di Capua Books. Imprint of Farrar, Straus and Giroux. Distributed by The Putnam Publishing Group, 390 Murray Hill Parkway, East Rutherford, NJ 07073, ATTN: Mail Order Department (for individual orders) or ATTN: Order Editing (for school or library orders).

Dial Books. Division of E. P. Dutton. Orders to: Penguin USA, 375 Hudson Street, New York, NY 10014.

Dial Books for Young Readers. Division of E. P. Dutton. Orders to: Penguin USA, 375 Hudson Street, New York, NY 10014.

Dillon Press, 242 Portland Avenue South, Minneapolis, MN 55415.

Dodd, Mead and Company has gone out of business. Some of their titles are being distributed by Siena Publishers' Associates, 45 West 36th Street, New York, NY 10018. Call first (1-800-223-0282) to see if the title you are interested in is available.

Doubleday. Division of Bantam Doubleday Dell Publishing Group, 666 Fifth Avenue, New York, NY 10103.

E. P. Dutton. Division of Penguin USA, 375 Hudson Street, New York, NY 10014.

M. Evans and Company. Distributed by Little, Brown and Company. Orders to: 200 West Street, Waltham, MA 02154.

Farrar, Straus and Giroux. Distributed by The Putnam Publishing Group, 390 Murray Hill Parkway, East Rutherford, NJ 07073, ATTN: Mail Order Department (for individual orders) or ATTN: Order Editing (for school or library orders).

Fawcett Juniper Books. Imprint of Random House. Orders to: 400 Hahn Road, Westminster, MD 21157.

Four Winds Press. Imprint of Macmillan Publishing Company. Orders to: Riverside Distribution Center, Front and Brown Streets, Riverside, NJ 08075.

Gemstone Books. Imprint of Dillon Press, 242 Portland Avenue South, Minneapolis, MN 55415.

Greenwillow Books. Division of William Morrow and Company. Orders to: 39 Plymouth Street, P.O. Box 1219, Fairfield, NJ 07007.

Harcourt Brace Jovanovich. Orders to: 465 South Lincoln Drive, Troy, MO 63379.

Harper and Row, Publishers. Orders to: Keystone Industrial Park, Scranton, PA 18512.

Harper Keypoint Books. Imprint of Harper and Row Junior Books. Orders to: Keystone Industrial Park, Scranton, PA 18512.

High Noon Books. Imprint of Academic Therapy Publications, 20 Commercial Boulevard, Novato, CA 94949.

Holiday House, 18 East 53rd Street, New York, NY 10022.

Henry Holt and Company. Orders to: Order Department, P.O. Box 30135, Salt Lake City, UT 84130.

Houghton Mifflin Company. Orders to: Wayside Road, Burlington, MA 01803.

Joy Street Books. Imprint of Little, Brown and Company. Orders to: 200 West Street, Waltham, MA 02154.

Alfred A. Knopf. Subsidiary of Random House. Orders to: 400 Hahn Road, Westminster, MD 21157.

Landmark Books, 260 Fifth Avenue, New York, NY 10001.

Laurel-Leaf Books. Imprint of Dell Publishing Company, division of Bantam Doubleday Dell Publishing Group, 666 Fifth Avenue, New York, NY 10103.

Lerner Publications, 241 First Avenue North, Minneapolis, MN 55401.

Directory of Publishers

J. B. Lippincott. Subsidiary of Harper and Row, Publishers. Orders to: Keystone Industrial Park, Scranton, PA 18512.

Little, Brown and Company. Division of Time, Inc. Orders to: 200 West Street, Waltham, MA 02154.

Lodestar Books. Imprint of E. P. Dutton. Orders to: Penguin USA, 375 Hudson Street, New York, NY 10014.

Lothrop, Lee and Shepard Books. Division of William Morrow and Company. Orders to: 39 Plymouth Street, Fairfield, NJ 07006.

Macmillan Publishing Company. Orders to: Riverside Distribution Center, Front and Brown Streets, Riverside, NJ 08075.

Margaret K. McElderry Books. Imprint of Macmillan Publishing Company. Orders to: Riverside Distribution Center, Front and Brown Streets, Riverside, NJ 08075.

Julian Messner. Division of Silver Burdett Press. Orders to: P.O. Box 2649, Columbus, OH 43216.

Metropolitan Museum of Art. Orders to: Special Services Office, Flushing, NY 11381.

William Morrow and Company. Orders to: Wilmor Warehouse, P.O. Box 1219, 39 Plymouth Street, Fairfield, NJ 07007.

Morrow Junior Books. Imprint of William Morrow and Company. Orders to: 39 Plymouth Street, Fairfield, NJ 07007.

Orchard Books. Imprint of Franklin Watts. Orders to: P.O. Box 1726, Danbury, CT 06816.

Owl Books. Imprint of Henry Holt and Company. Orders to: Order Department, P.O. Box 30135, Salt Lake City, UT 84130.

Philomel Books. Imprint of The Putnam Publishing Group, 390 Murray Hill Parkway, East Rutherford, NJ 07073, ATTN: Mail Order Department (for individual orders) or ATTN: Order Editing (for school or library orders).

Prentice Hall Books for Young Readers. Imprint of Simon and Schuster. Orders to: 200 Old Tappan Road, Old Tappan, NJ 07675.

G. P. Putnam's Sons. Division of The Putnam Publishing Group, 390 Murray Hill Parkway, East Rutherford, NJ 07073, ATTN: Mail Order Department (for individual orders) or ATTN: Order Editing (for school or library orders).

Random House. Orders to: 400 Hahn Road, Westminster, MD 21157.

St. Martin's Press, 175 Fifth Avenue, New York, NY 10010.

Scholastic. Orders to: 2931 East McCarty Street, Jefferson City, MO 65102.

Charles Scribner's Sons. Imprint of Macmillan Publishing Company. Orders to: Riverside Distribution Center, Front and Brown Streets, Riverside, NJ 08075.

Sierra Club Books. Distributed by Random House, 400 Hahn Road, Westminster, MD 21157.

Silver Burdett Press. Subsidiary of Simon and Schuster. Order to: P.O. Box 2649, Columbus, OH 43216.

Simon and Schuster Books for Young Readers. Imprint of Simon and Schuster. Orders to: 200 Old Tappan Road, Old Tappan, NJ 07675.

Sterling Publishing Company, 387 Park Avenue South, New York, NY 10016-8810.

Vintage Books. Imprint of Random House, 400 Hahn Road, Westminster, MD 21157.

Walker Publishing Company, 720 Fifth Avenue, New York, NY 10019.

Franklin Watts. Subsidiary of Grolier. Orders to: P.O. Box 1726, Danbury, CT 06816.

Wesleyan University Press. Orders to: Box 702, Wolfeboro, NH 03894-0702.

Author Index

Aaseng, Nathan, 3.1, 3.2, 3.3, 13.1
Adler, C. S., 6.1, 6.2
Aiken, Joan, 23.1
Alexander, Lloyd, 1.1, 1.2
Anderson, Dave, 22.1
Anderson, Joan, 13.2
Armitage, Ronda, 24.1
Asch, Frank, 20.1
Auch, Mary Jane, 6.3, 6.4, 6.5
Avi, 17.1

Babbitt, Natalie, 8.1
Banks, Lynne Reid, 7.1
Barnes, Jeremy, 3.4
Beatty, John, 24.2
Beatty, Patricia, 12.1
Becerra de Jenkins, Lyll, 21.1
Bedard, Michael, 23.2
Behrens, Michael, 10.1
Bell, William, 10.2
Bellairs, John, 17.2
Bennett, Jay, 17.3, 17.4
Berger, Gilda, 21.2
Berger, Melvin, 19.1
Betancourt, Jeanne, 6.6, 9.1
Bevan, Nicholas, 11.1
Bix, Cynthia Overbeck, 24.14
Black, Sheila, 3.5
Blackwood, Gary L., 20.2
Blair, Cynthia, 20.3
Bleifeld, Maurice, 19.2
Block, Francesca Lia, 10.3
Blume, Judy, 9.2
Boehm, David A., 22.2
Borton de Treviño, Elizabeth, 1.3
Bottner, Barbara, 10.4
Boutis, Victoria, 6.7
Bowman, John, 3.6
Boyd, Candy Dawson, 10.5
Brandt, Sue R., 14.1
Branley, Franklyn M., 19.3
Branscum, Robbie, 17.5
Brooks, Bruce, 20.4
Brown, Fern G., 17.6
Buranelli, Vincent, 3.7

Busselle, Rebecca, 10.6
Butler, Bonnie, 10.7

Calvert, Patricia, 10.8
Campbell, Hope, 17.7
Caraker, Mary, 20.5
Caras, Roger A., 2.1
Carey, M. V., 17.8, 17.9
Carkeet, David, 10.9
Carr, Jess, 1.4
Carter, Alden R., 4.1
Castiglia, Julie, 3.8
Chaikin, Miriam, 13.3
Chaple, Glenn F., Jr., 19.4
Charnas, Suzy McKee, 7.2, 7.3
Childress, Alice, 21.3
Christiansen, C. B., 10.10
Christopher, John, 20.6
Cobb, Vicki, 19.5
Cohen, Barbara, 5.1
Cole, Brock, 10.11, 10.12
Collier, James Lincoln, 6.8, 21.4
Conford, Ellen, 16.1, 23.3
Conrad, Pam, 12.2
Coombs, Charles, 22.3
Cooney, Caroline B., 10.13, 16.2, 16.3
Corcoran, Barbara, 6.9, 10.14
Corning, Josie, 24.3
Crofford, Emily, 19.6
Cross, Gillian, 9.3
Crutcher, Chris, 21.5, 22.4
Cunningham, Marilyn, 23.4
Currey, Richard, 10.15
Cusick, Richie Tankersley, 17.10
Cwiklik, Robert, 3.9, 3.10

Daneman, Meredith, 10.16
Danziger, Paula, 6.10
Davis, Jenny, 10.17
Davis, Leila, 16.4
Deegan, Paul J., 24.4, 24.5
Deuker, Carl, 22.5
Dexter, Catherine, 7.4
Diggs, Lucy, 2.2
Dines, Carol, 6.11

121

Dinner, Sherry H., 11.2
Douglas, Marjie, 23.5
Downing, Warwick, 1.5
Draper, C. G., 15.1
Duden, Jane, 13.4
Dudman, John, 13.5
Duffy, James, 17.11
Duggleby, John, 19.7
Dunbar, Robert E., 14.2
Duncan, Lois, 17.12, 17.13
Dunlop, Eileen, 17.14, 23.6
Dunnahoo, Terry, 19.8
Dygard, Thomas J., 22.6

Ehrlich, Amy, 6.12
Einhorn, Barbara, 24.6
Eisenberg, Lisa, 17.15, 17.16
Elfman, Blossom, 16.5
Ethridge, Kenneth E., 9.4

Faber, Doris, 3.11, 13.6
Faber, Harold, 3.11, 13.6
Farrell, Kate, 18.6
Ferris, Jean, 4.2
Feuer, Elizabeth, 10.18
Filichia, Peter, 5.2
Fine, Anne, 6.13, 21.6
Fisher, Dorothy Canfield, 13.7
Fisher, Leonard Everett, 13.8
Fleischman, Paul, 18.1
Forman, James D., 21.7
Fornatale, Pete, 13.9
Fosburgh, Liza, 6.14
Fowler, Virginie, 14.3
Fradin, Dennis Brindell, 3.12
Freedman, Russell, 3.13, 3.14
French, Michael, 10.19
Furlong, Monica, 7.5

Gabhart, Ann, 23.7
Gaeddert, LouAnn, 6.15
Garden, Nancy, 7.6
Gates, Susan, 23.8
George, Jean Craighead, 10.20
Gibbons, Faye, 9.5
Gilbert, Sara D., 11.3
Gilden, Mel, 20.7
Gillies, John, 3.15
Gilson, Jamie, 15.2
Glassman, Bruce S., 3.16
Glenn, Mel, 18.2
Glover, Vivian, 5.3
Gondosch, Linda, 9.6
Gordon, Sheila, 5.4
Graff, Nancy Price, 6.16
Grafton, Sue, 17.17

Grant, Cynthia D., 4.3
Green, Carl R., 19.19, 19.20
Green, Connie Jordan, 6.17
Gregory, Lee, 24.7

Hahn, Mary Downing, 6.18
Halam, Ann, 7.7
Hall, Lynn, 10.21, 17.18, 17.19, 23.9
Hallman, Ruth, 1.6
Hamilton, Virginia, 3.17, 21.8
Harrar, George, 19.9
Harrar, Linda, 19.9
Harris, Jonathan, 22.7
Harris, Mark Jonathan, 21.9
Haynes, Betsy, 16.6
Henken, Heidi, 1.7
Henry, Maeve, 7.8
Henry, Sondra, 24.11
Herberman, Ethan, 2.3
Heuck, Sigrid, 12.3
Hildick, E. W., 17.20, 23.10
Hinton, S. E., 10.22
Hobbs, Will, 6.19
Holbrook, Sabra, 21.10
Holl, Kristi D., 10.23, 10.24
Holland, Isabelle, 17.21, 17.22
Hoobler, Thomas, 20.8
Hooper, Nancy J., 10.25
Hopkins, Lila, 2.4
Hoppe, Joanne, 9.7
Horn, Gabriel, 19.10
Howard, Elizabeth, 17.23, 17.24, 17.25, 17.26
Hurwitz, Johanna, 17.27
Husted, Darrell, 6.20

Ireland, Karin, 3.18
Irwin, Hadley, 4.4
Isberg, Emily, 19.11

Jacques, Brian, 7.9
Janeczko, Paul B., 18.3, 18.4
Jaspersohn, William, 17.28
Jensen, Kathryn, 6.21
Johnson, Neil, 3.19
Johnson, Norma Tadlock, 7.10
Johnston, Norma, 17.29
Jones, Rebecca C., 6.22
Jones, Robin D., 10.26
Jurmain, Suzanne, 2.5

Kaplow, Robert, 16.7
Kettelkamp, Larry, 19.12
Kidd, Ronald, 17.30
Kirshenbaum, Binnie, 10.27
Klass, David, 10.28, 22.8

Author Index

Klass, Sheila Solomon, 6.23, 6.24
Klein, Norma, 6.25, 9.8
Knudson, R. R., 18.5, 22.9
Koch, Kenneth, 18.6
Koertge, Ron, 10.29
Kolodny, Nancy J., 11.4
Komunyakaa, Yusef, 18.7
Korman, Gordon, 15.3

Landis, J. D., 10.30
Lasky, Kathryn, 5.5
Lawson, Don, 13.10
Lee, Sally, 19.13
Lester, Julius, 8.2
Levitin, Sonia, 5.6
Logan, Carolyn F., 7.11
Lomask, Milton, 3.20
Lowry, Lois, 5.7

Mahoney, Mary Reeves, 6.26
Mahy, Margaret, 10.31
Major, Kevin, 10.32
Makris, Kathryn, 16.8
Malmgren, Dallin, 21.11
Manes, Stephen, 15.4, 15.5, 15.6
Mango, Karin N., 10.33
Marek, Margot, 22.10
Marsden, John, 6.27
Matas, Carol, 12.4
Math, Irwin, 19.14
Matthews, Phoebe, 10.34, 16.9
Maurer, Richard, 19.15
Mauser, Pat Rhoads, 2.6
Mazer, Harry, 4.5, 16.10
Mazer, Norma Fox, 4.5
McClard, Megan, 3.21
McFann, Jane, 10.35, 10.36
McGowen, Tom, 7.12
McGraw, Eloise, 23.11
McKenzie, Ellen Kindt, 7.13
McKinley, Robin, 8.3
McWhirter, Norris, 13.14
Mell, Jan, 19.16
Meltzer, Milton, 13.11, 13.12
Miklowitz, Gloria D., 10.37, 21.12, 22.11
Miller, W. Wesley, 17.31, 23.12
Morris, Winifred, 21.13
Morrison, Susan Dudley, 19.17
Morton, Jane, 21.14
Moulton, Deborah, 7.14
Mullin, Penn, 10.38, 20.9
Murphy, Jim, 14.4
Murrow, Liza Ketchum, 17.32

Namovicz, Gene Inyart, 10.39
Naylor, Phyllis Reynolds, 6.28

Neimark, Anne E., 3.22
Nelson, Ginger K., 17.33
Nesnick, Victoria Gilvary, 3.23
Nielsen, Nancy J., 24.8
Nixon, Joan Lowery, 12.5, 17.34, 17.35
Norman, Howard, 8.4

Pageler, Elaine, 23.13
Paisner, Daniel, 10.52
Patent, Dorothy Hinshaw, 2.7
Paterson, Katherine, 6.29
Paulsen, Gary, 1.8, 1.9, 6.30, 10.40
Pearce, Q. L., 19.18
Pearson, Gayle, 12.6
Peck, Richard, 23.14
Peck, Robert Newton, 15.7, 21.15
Pelta, Kathy, 3.24
Pendergraft, Patricia, 10.41
Perl, Lila, 13.13
Petersen, P. J., 1.10
Pfeffer, Susan Beth, 6.31, 6.32, 16.11, 20.10
Pike, Christopher, 17.36
Pinsker, Judith, 9.9
Pitts, Paul, 5.8
Pople, Maureen, 10.42
Posner, Richard, 7.15, 16.12
Price, Susan, 7.16
Pringle, Laurence, 11.5

Rabe, Berniece, 10.43
Radford, Ken, 23.15
Ramusi, Molapatene Collins, 3.25
Regan, Dian Curtis, 1.11
Riding, Julia, 20.11
Rochman, Hazel, 5.9
Rodda, Emily, 7.17
Rodowsky, Colby, 6.33
Rostkowski, Margaret I., 9.10
Roth-Hano, Renée, 5.10
Ruby, Lois, 10.44
Ruckman, Ivy, 1.12
Russell, Alan, 13.14
Ryan, Margaret, 14.5
Ryan, Mary C., 10.45, 10.46
Rylant, Cynthia, 6.34

Samuels, Gertrude, 21.16
Sanford, William R., 19.19, 19.20
Santini, Rosemarie, 16.13
Sattler, Helen Roney, 2.8
Saville, Lynn, 2.9
Scariano, Margaret, 6.35
Schmitt, Lois, 14.6
Schwandt, Stephen, 4.6
Scott, Elaine, 22.12
Seidler, Tor, 7.18

Seixas, Judith S., 21.17
Selden, George, 7.19
Service, Pamela F., 1.13, 7.20, 20.12
Seuling, Barbara, 11.6
Shachtman, Tom, 2.10
Shannon, George, 6.36
Shaw, Diana, 17.37
Shorto, Russell, 3.26, 3.27
Shreve, Susan, 17.38
Shusterman, Neal, 17.39
Shyer, Marlene Fanta, 10.47
Silver, Donald M., 2.11
Silverstein, Herma, 23.16
Singer, Marilyn, 6.37
Slepian, Jan, 10.48
Smirnoff, Yakov, 15.8
Snyder, Carol, 6.38
Snyder, Zilpha Keatley, 17.40
Sobol, Donald J., 15.9
Spinelli, Jerry, 9.11
Spremich, Andrew, 20.13
Springer, Nancy, 2.12
Sproule, Anna, 24.9
Stephenson, Sallie, 24.10
Strasser, Todd, 10.49, 21.18
Sufrin, Mark, 3.28
Sullivan, George, 3.29, 3.30, 13.15, 22.13
Sutton, Jane, 10.50
Swenson, May, 18.5
Swindells, Robert, 21.19
Symes, R. F., 19.21

Taitz, Emily, 24.11
Tapp, Kathy Kennedy, 21.20
Tate, Eleanora E., 5.11
Terris, Susan, 12.7

Tolan, Stephanie S., 1.14, 15.10
Tompert, Ann, 3.31
Townsend, John Rowe, 1.15
Trudeau, G. B., 15.11
Turck, May, 24.12, 24.13
Turner, Ruth S., 3.25

Van Oosting, James, 23.17
Vedral, Joyce L., 16.14

Wagoner, David, 18.8
Walker, Mary Alexander, 10.51
Wallace, Bill, 1.16, 2.13, 17.41
Wallin, Luke, 5.12
Warner, Malcolm-Jamal, 10.52
Weidhorn, Manfred, 3.32
Weller, Frances Ward, 6.39
Wells, Rosemary, 7.21
Wersba, Barbara, 21.21
Whitehead, Victoria, 23.18
Wilson, A. N., 2.14
Wisler, G. Clifton, 5.13
Wolff, Virginia Euwer, 21.22
Wright, Betty Ren, 23.19
Wrightson, Patricia, 23.20
Wyss, Thelma Hatch, 10.53

Yolen, Jane, 7.22, 7.23
Young, Donald, 24.14
Ypsilantis, George, 3.21

Zable, Rona S., 16.15
Zalben, Jane Breskin, 9.12
Zelazny, Roger, 7.24
Zindel, Paul, 4.7

Title Index

Abraham Lincoln Brigade, The: Americans Fighting Fascism in the Spanish Civil War, 13.10
Accident, The, 21.18
AIDS and Drugs, 11.1
Albert Einstein, 3.18
Alessandra in Love, 16.7
Alexander Graham Bell, 3.24
Alias Madame Doubtfire, 6.13
All in a Day's Work: Twelve Americans Talk about Their Jobs, 3.19
America on Six Rubles a Day; or, How to Become a Capitalist Pig, 15.8
American Politics: How It Really Works, 13.11
American Sports Poems, 18.5
Among Friends, 10.13
Andrew Carnegie: Steel Tycoon, 3.6
Animal World, The, 2.11
Animals in Their Places: Tales from the Natural World, 2.1
Anthony Burns: The Defeat and Triumph of a Fugitive Slave, 3.17
Anything to Win, 22.11
Arizona Kid, The, 10.29
Arly, 21.15
At the Edge, 10.1
Atlantic Gray Whale, The, 19.16

Baby-Sitter on Horseback, 17.6
Balyet, 23.20
Band Never Dances, The, 10.30
Bathing Ugly, 10.6
Bats on the Bedstead, 7.10
Be Ever Hopeful, Hannalee, 12.1
Beansprouts, 16.13
Begonia for Miss Applebaum, A, 4.7
Believers, The, 6.22
Best Friends Tell the Best Lies, 6.11
Best of Friends, The, 9.10
Big League Spring Training, 22.13
Birth of a Nation, The: The Early Years of the United States, 13.6
Blain's Woods, 17.31
Boat Song, 6.39

Bone Wars, The, 5.5
Book of Eagles, The, 2.8
Boundary Waters Canoe Area, Minnesota, 24.8
Boy on the Cover, The, 16.9
Brad's Box, 10.51
Breakaway Run, 10.28
Brickyard Summer, 18.3
Bronze King, The, 7.2
Burnhope Wheel, The, 23.8

Cameo Rose, 17.5
Camp Girl-Meets-Boy, 16.2
Carrie's Games, 10.25
Case of the Savage Statue, The, 17.8
Celine, 10.11
Cellar, The, 23.15
Ceremony of the Panther, 5.12
Changes in Latitudes, 6.19
Charlie Pippin, 10.5
Ché! Latin America's Legendary Guerilla Leader, 3.22
Chicago, Illinois, 24.12
Chicken Trek: The Third Strange Thing That Happened to Oscar Noodleman, 15.4
Chimney Witch Chase, 23.18
Chinese Handcuffs, 21.5
Choices, 22.12
City Kid's Field Guide, The, 2.3
Class Dismissed II: More High School Poems, 18.2
Clayworks: Colorful Crafts around the World, 14.3
Cobb's Cave, 1.7
Cold and Hot Winter, The, 17.27
Come the Morning, 21.9
Coming Home Cafe, The, 12.6
Computer Graphics: How It Works, What It Does, 19.12
Crabbe's Journey, 10.2
Crazy Horse Electric Game, The, 22.4
Credit-Card Carole, 6.23
Crossing, The, 10.40
Cruise Control, 6.14

125

Cry Havoc, 21.7
Cry Uncle!, 6.3
Custom Car: A Nuts-and-Bolts Guide to Creating One, 14.4

Dagmar Schultz and the Powers of Darkness, 23.9
Dancer in the Mirror, 21.13
Danger in Quicksand Swamp, 17.41
Dark and Deadly Pool, The, 17.34
Dark Corridor, The, 17.3
Dark Secret, The, 23.12
Darker Magic, A, 23.2
Dear Bruce Springsteen: A Novel, 10.32
Deathtrap and Dinosaur, 10.35
Definitely Not Sexy, 10.50
Denver, Colorado, 24.3
Devil's Other Storybook, The, 8.1
Dien Cai Dau, 18.7
Different Way, A, 16.8
Dodo, The, 19.19
Don't Look behind You, 17.12
Donor Banks: Saving Lives with Organ and Tissue Transplants, 19.13
Door Between, The, 7.6
Downtown Doonesbury, 15.11
Dr. Chill's Project, 20.8
Drackenberg Adventure, The, 1.1
Dreaming, 10.7
Drugged Athletes: The Crisis in American Sports, 22.7
Dump Days, 9.11
Dying Sun, The, 20.2

Earthborn: In Celebration of Wild Places, 24.2
Eating Crow, 2.4
El Dorado Adventure, The, 1.2
El Güero: A True Adventure Story, 1.3
Encyclopedia Brown's Book of Wacky Cars, 15.9
Evvie at Sixteen, 16.11
Experimenting with a Microscope, 19.2
Exploring with a Telescope, 19.4
Eyes of the Killer Robot, The, 17.2

"F" Is for Fugitive, 17.17
Faery Flag, The: Stories and Poems of Fantasy and the Supernatural, 7.22
Fairy Rebel, The, 7.1
Family Apart, A, 12.5
Fatal Light, 10.15
Fighting Back: The Struggle for Gay Rights, 21.10
Fire in the Heart, 17.32
First Battle of Morn, The, 7.14

First Fig Tree, The, 5.3
First Love Lives Forever, 16.5
Fitchett's Folly, 6.33
Flight of the Dragon, 20.13
Following the Mystery Man, 6.18
Fortunate Fortunes, The, 3.1
Fortunate Isles, The, 1.15
Forward Pass, 22.6
Francie and the Boys, 10.16
Frankie's Run, 10.45
Freedom to Dream, 20.3

Game of Survival, 1.11
Genie with the Light Blue Hair, 23.3
Geronimo and the Struggle for Apache Freedom, 3.26
Get Help: Solving the Problems in Your Life, 11.3
Ghost Drum, The: A Cat's Tale, 7.16
Ghost in the Window, A, 23.19
Ghost Squad and the Menace of the Malevs, The, 23.10
Ghost Squad and the Prowling Hermits, The, 17.20
Ghosts of Black Point, The, 10.38
Girl of His Dreams, The, 16.10
Girl Who Invented Romance, The, 16.3
Give Yourself a Fright: Thirteen Tales of the Supernatural, 23.1
Glass Slippers Give You Blisters, 6.4
Goats, The, 10.12
Going Over to Your Place: Poems for Each Other, 18.4
Good-Bye Tomorrow, 10.37
Goodnight, Cinderella, 16.12
Great Ancestor Hunt, The: The Fun of Finding Out Who You Are, 13.13
Great Auk, The, 19.6
Great Boyfriend Trap, The, 16.6
Great Britain, 24.9
Great Gerbil Roundup, The, 15.5
Great Lives: American Government, 3.11
Great Lives: Exploration, 3.20
Great Lives: Sports, 3.29
Great Skinner Getaway, The, 15.10
Great Skinner Homestead, The, 1.14
Greatest Showman on Earth, The: A Biography of P. T. Barnum, 3.31
Grounded, 17.28

Harry Newberry and the Raiders of the Red Drink, 20.7
Hatchet, 1.8
Haunted One, The, 17.4
Heartbeat, 4.5
Here at the Scenic-Vu Motel, 10.53

Title Index

Hiawatha and the Iroquois League, 3.21
Hidden in the Fog, 10.23
Hideaway, The, 10.14
Hideout, The, 12.3
Hobie Hanson, You're Weird, 15.2
Holding Steady, 4.6
Holiday Year, A, 15.1
Home Sweet Home, 6.6
Honorable Prison, The, 21.1
Horses in the Circus Ring, 2.9
House on the Hill, The, 17.14
How Can You Hijack a Cave?, 1.10
"How Glooskap Outwits the Ice Giants" and Other Tales of the Maritime Indians, 8.4
How the White House Really Works, 13.15
How to Debate, 14.2
How to Write a Report, 14.1
Hurry-up Summer, The, 6.26

I Am Phoenix: Poems for Two Voices, 18.1
If You Need Me, 6.1
Indian Chiefs, 3.13
Intruder in the Wind, 1.4
Invincible Summer, 4.2
Island, The, 1.9
Island of Dangerous Dreams, The, 17.35
Israel: A Sacred Land, 24.11

J. Paul Getty: Oil Billionaire, 3.16
Janie's Private Eyes, 17.40
Journey to Terezor, 20.1
Junk in Space, 19.15
Just as Long as We're Together, 9.2

Kashka, 7.13
Kid Curry's Last Ride, 1.5
Killing Freeze, A, 17.18
Kindness, A, 6.34
King Philip and the War with the Colonists, 3.9
King Shoes and Clown Pockets, 9.5

Last Act, 17.36
Leave Me Alone, Ma, 6.38
Leaving, The, 10.21
Lessons in Fear, 17.37
Let Me Tell You Everything: Memoirs of a Lovesick Intellectual, 10.4
Lifeguard, The, 17.10
Lincoln: A Photobiography, 3.14
Lisa's War, 12.4
Living in a Risky World, 11.5
Living with a Parent Who Takes Drugs, 21.17

Looking for Hamlet: A Haunting at Deeping Lake, 17.7
Looking Out, 6.7
Los Angeles, California, 24.7
Lost Parrots of America, The, 19.8
Lot Like You, A, 9.9
Love at the Laundromat, 16.15
Love Is for the Dogs, 2.6
Lover Boy, 16.4
Lucy Forever and Miss Rosetree, Shrinks, 17.38

Mad, Mad Monday, 23.16
Magician's Company, The, 7.12
Map of Nowhere, A, 9.3
Margaret Mead, 3.8
Matrix Witch, 23.5
Matt's Crusade, 22.10
Maxie's Ghost, 23.17
Mazemaker, 7.4
Me and Joey Pinstripe, the King of Rock, 10.47
Memory, 10.31
Message from Outer Space, 20.9
Mikhail Gorbachev, 3.30
Miracle at Clement's Pond, 10.41
Missing, 17.11
Moon in the Water, 2.2
More Tales of Uncle Remus: Further Adventures of Brer Rabbit, His Friends, Enemies, and Others, 8.2
Murder at the Spaniel Show, 17.19
My Daniel, 12.2
My Life as a Body, 9.8
My War with Goggle-eyes, 21.6
Mysteries of Life on Earth and Beyond, 19.3
Mystery at Bluff Point Dunes, 17.15
Mystery at Snowshoe Mountain Lodge, 17.16
Mystery of the Cranky Collector, The, 17.9
Mystery of the Deadly Diamond, 17.23
Mystery of the Magician, 17.24
Mystery of the Metro, 17.25

Nashville, Tennessee, 24.4
Nell's Quilt, 12.7
New York, New York, 24.5
New Zealand, 24.1
Nightmare in History, A: The Holocaust 1933–1945, 13.3
1988 Guinness Book of World Records, 13.14
1989–90 Guinness Sports Record Book, 22.2
1940s, 13.4

Ninth Issue, The, 21.11
No Kidding, 20.4
No Place for Cal, 21.14
No Shakespeare Allowed, 10.26
No Strings Attached, 10.24
No Way Out, 1.12
Not Just Party Girls, 9.1
Not on a White Horse, 2.12
Nothing to Be Ashamed Of: Growing Up with Mental Illness in Your Family, 11.2
Now That I Know, 6.25
Nugget of Gold, A, 10.42
Number the Stars, 5.7

Obnoxious Jerks, The, 15.6
Old Meadow, The, 7.19
On the Devil's Court, 22.5
Once upon a Horse: A History of Horses—and How They Shaped Our History, 2.5
One Friend to Another, 10.18
One More Chance, 10.36
One Sister Too Many, 6.2
Opposite Sex Is Driving Me Crazy, The, 16.14
Orlando, Florida, 24.10
Our Independence and the Constitution, 13.7
Outlaws of Sherwood, The, 8.3
Outside Looking In, 6.8

Page Four, 6.24
Park's Quest, 6.29
Passenger Pigeon, The, 19.17
Payton, 3.28
Peak Performance: Sports, Science, and the Body in Action, 19.11
People Like Us, 5.1
Perfect Family, A, 6.20
Phoenix Rising; or, How to Survive Your Life, 4.3
Pick of the Litter, 6.5
Pig-Out Inn, 10.44
Pigs Are Flying!, The, 7.17
Pirate's Revenge, The, 17.33
Place of Power, A, 23.4
Pocket Change, 6.21
Power of the Rellard, The, 7.11
Pretty Penny Farm, 9.7
Princess Diana: A Book of Questions and Answers, 3.23
Probably Still Nick Swansen, 21.22
Problem Solvers, The, 3.2

Question of Destiny, A, 20.12

Quicksand and Other Earthly Wonders, 19.18

Racing the Sun, 5.8
Red Dog, 1.16
Redwall, 7.9
Rehearsal for the Bigtime, 10.43
Rejects, The, 13.1
Reluctant God, The, 1.13
Remarkable Children: Twenty Who Made History, 3.12
Remember Me to Harold Square, 6.10
Return to Morocco, 17.29
Rewind to Yesterday, 20.10
Rinehart Shouts, 22.9
Robert E. Lee, 3.32
Rocks and Minerals, 19.21
Runaway Magic, 23.13

Sabertooth Cat, The, 19.7
Sacred Circle of the Hula Hoop, The, 21.20
Samuel Goldwyn: Movie Mogul, 3.4
San Francisco Earthquake, The, 13.5
Scent of Murder, A, 17.26
Science of Music, The, 19.1
Search without Fear, 1.6
Second Fiddle: A Sizzle and Splat Mystery, 17.30
Secret of Gumbo Grove, The, 5.11
Secrets Not Meant to Be Kept, 21.12
Semester in the Life of a Garbage Bag, A, 15.3
Sending of Dragons, A, 7.23
Señor Alcalde: A Biography of Henry Cisneros, 3.15
Sequoyah and the Cherokee Alphabet, 3.10
Serpent's Tooth, A, 21.19
Several Kinds of Silence, 6.37
Sex Education, 10.17
Shadow Club, The, 17.39
Shark beneath the Reef, 10.20
Sheila's Dying, 4.1
Short Subject, 10.27
Sierra Club Book of Our National Parks, The, 24.14
Sign of Chaos, 7.24
Signs of the Apes, Songs of the Whales: Adventures in Human-Animal Communication, 19.9
Silent Treatment, The, 10.9
Silver Days, 5.6
Silver Glove, The, 7.3
Sitting Bull and the Battle of the Little Bighorn, 3.5

Small Pleasure, A, 10.10
Smart Spending: A Young Consumer's Guide, 14.6
Snot Stew, 2.13
Snows of Jaspre, The, 20.5
So Long at the Fair, 4.4
So Much to Tell You . . ., 6.27
So You Have to Give a Speech!, 14.5
Soaring: Where Hawks and Eagles Fly, 22.3
Somehow Tenderness Survives: Stories of Southern Africa, 5.9
Something beyond Paradise, 10.48
Somewhere Green, 10.33
Soup's Uncle, 15.7
Soweto, My Love, 3.25
Space Traders Unlimited, 20.11
Spanish Pioneers of the Southwest, 13.2
Sparrow's Flight, 7.15
Steller's Sea Cow, 19.10
Story of Basketball, The, 22.1
Story of Rock 'n' Roll, The, 13.9
Stranger, You and I, 10.8
Stray, 2.14
Strength of the Hills, The: A Portrait of a Family Farm, 6.16
Summer Like Turnips, A, 6.15
Summer Strike Out, 6.35
Switchstance, 10.34

Talking to the Sun: An Illustrated Anthology of Poems for Young People, 18.6
Taming the Star Runner, 10.22
Tar Pit, The, 7.18
Tecumseh and the Dream of an American Indian Nation, 3.27
Thea at Sixteen, 6.31
Theo and Me: Growing Up Okay, 10.52
Thief, 17.21
Things I Did for Love, The, 16.1
Thomas Alva Edison, 3.7
Those Other People, 21.3
Through the Forest: New and Selected Poems, 1977–1987, 18.8
Through the Hidden Door, 7.21
To Talk in Time, 10.39
Touch Wood: A Girlhood in Occupied France, 5.10
Transformations, 7.7
Trouble with Jacob, The, 23.11
Twisted Window, The, 17.13

Unfrightened Dark, The, 17.22
Unlived Affections, 6.36
Unsung Heroes, The, 3.3
Us against Them, 10.19

USA for Africa: Rock Aid in the Eighties, 21.2

Valley of Deer, The, 23.6
Viola, Furgy, Bobbi, and Me, 9.4
Voices after Midnight, 23.14
Voices from the Civil War: A Documentary History of the Great American Conflict, 13.12

Waiting for the Rain: A Novel of South Africa, 5.4
War at Home, The, 6.17
Washington, D.C., 24.13
Water from the Moon, 9.12
Wavebender: A Story of Daniel au Fond, 2.10
Weetzie Bat, 10.3
West Germany, 24.6
What's in a Name?, 5.2
When Food's a Foe: How to Confront and Conquer Eating Disorders, 11.4
When the Tripods Came, 20.6
Where It Stops, Nobody Knows, 6.12
Where the Wild Horses Roam, 2.7
White House, The, 13.8
White Romance, A, 21.8
Who Says I Can't, 10.46
Who's Afraid of Haggerty House?, 9.6
Why Doesn't the Earth Fall Up? And Other Not Such Dumb Questions about Motion, 19.5
Wildlife, 10.49
Winchesters, The, 21.4
Winter of Magic's Return, 7.20
Winter Room, The, 6.30
Wires and Watts: Understanding and Using Electricity, 19.14
Wise Child, 7.5
Wish Come True, 23.7
Witch King, The, 7.8
Wolf Rider: A Tale of Terror, 17.1
Wolf's Tooth, The, 5.13
Wonderful Me, 21.21
Woolly Mammoth, The, 19.20
Wrestling with Honor, 22.8

Year of the Gopher, The, 6.28
Year without Michael, The, 6.32
You Can't Sneeze with Your Eyes Open and Other Freaky Facts about the Human Body, 11.6
You Put Up with Me, I'll Put Up with You, 6.9
Yours, Brett, 21.16

Subject Index

Adoption, 6.5
Adventure and adventurers, 1.1–16
Advice for teens, 10.52, 16.14
African Americans, 3.17, 5.3, 5.11, 21.3, 21.8
AIDS, 10.37, 11.1
Alabama, 9.5
Alcoholism, 2.12, 6.14, 10.2, 20.4
Animal communication, 19.9
Animals, extinct, 19.6–8, 19.10, 19.16, 19.17, 19.19, 19.20
Animals, urban, 2.3
Animals, wild, 2.1, 2.7
Anthropologists, 3.8
Apartheid, 3.25, 5.4, 5.9
Archaeology, 5.5
Art and artists, 17.26, 18.6
Asian Americans, 6.29
Astronomy, 19.3, 19.4
Athletes, 3.28, 3.29, 22.7, 22.8
Aunts, 16.11, 17.14, 17.35
Australia, 6.27, 10.42, 23.20

Babies, 6.2, 6.5, 6.34, 10.41
Baseball, 9.4, 22.4, 22.13
Basketball, 22.1, 22.5
Bats, 7.10
Biology, 19.2
Birds, 2.4, 2.8, 18.1, 19.6, 19.8, 19.17, 19.19
Boating, 22.9
Brothers and sisters, 2.13, 6.5, 6.8, 6.10, 6.19, 10.30, 10.33, 12.2, 12.5, 21.5, 21.20
Buried treasure, 17.41
Business and businesspeople, 3.1–3, 3.6, 3.16, 13.1

California, 13.5, 24.7
Camping, 1.11, 10.19
Camps, 10.6, 10.12, 16.2
Cancer, 4.1–3, 4.7, 6.31
Careers, 3.19
Caring, 10.17
Cars, 14.4, 15.9
Cats, 2.13, 2.14

Central America, 1.2
Child abuse, 21.5
Child prodigies, 3.12
Circuses, 2.9, 3.31
Civil rights, 3.25, 21.10, 22.12
Civil War, U.S., 3.14, 3.32, 12.1, 13.12
Clubs, 15.6, 17.39
Colorado, 24.3
Comic books, 15.11, 20.7
Computers, 19.12
Constitution, U.S., 13.7
Consumer education, 14.6
Contests, 6.10, 10.6, 10.9, 15.3, 15.4
Courage, 1.16
Cousins, 6.17, 17.14
Crime, 1.5, 10.27, 10.44, 17.15, 23.11
Cults, 6.22, 10.48

Death, 4.1–7, 6.15, 6.36, 10.30, 10.31
Debating, 14.2
Declaration of Independence, 13.7
Denmark, 12.4
Depression, The, 12.6
Diaries, 4.3, 6.27, 10.13, 16.7
Dinosaurs, 5.5, 12.2
Divorce, 6.13, 6.24, 6.25, 10.1, 10.28, 10.32, 10.34, 10.36, 21.6, 21.16, 21.21
Dogs, 1.16, 2.6, 17.19
Dragons, 7.23
Dreams, 7.14, 17.33, 23.19
Drug abuse, 10.47, 10.49, 11.1, 21.17, 22.7, 22.8, 22.11
Drunk driving, 10.14, 21.18

Earthquakes, 13.5
Eating disorders, 11.4
Electricity, 19.14
Emotional problems, 6.11, 6.27, 10.1, 10.31, 10.39, 10.40, 12.7, 17.13, 17.21, 17.38
Entertainers, 3.4, 3.31, 10.52
Environmental health, 11.5
Ethnic identity, 5.2
Exchange students, 6.6, 10.28
Explorers, 3.20

Fairies, 7.1
Family life, 1.14, 4.3, 5.3, 6.1–39, 9.2, 10.8, 10.9, 10.21, 10.23, 15.1, 15.10, 17.32, 17.40, 20.4
Fantasy, 7.1–24
Fantasy games, 7.15, 9.3
Farm life, 6.3, 6.6, 6.16, 6.29, 6.30, 10.21, 10.51
Fathers and daughters, 6.1, 6.18, 6.25, 6.26, 6.31, 10.5, 10.25, 10.26
Fathers and sons, 4.6, 6.39, 17.1
Feminism, 10.4
Fishing, 10.20
Florida, 21.15, 24.10
Folktales, 8.1, 8.2
Football, 3.28, 22.6, 22.10, 22.11
Foster homes, 12.5, 21.14, 21.16
France, 17.23–26
Freedom of speech, 21.1, 21.11
Friendship, 2.4, 2.6, 4.2, 4.4, 4.5, 5.4, 5.13, 6.6, 6.9–11, 6.31, 7.15, 7.18, 7.20, 9.1–12, 10.3, 10.9, 10.13, 10.14, 10.16, 10.40, 10.42, 10.45, 15.2, 15.3, 16.6, 17.27, 21.8, 21.13
Frontier and pioneer life, 1.16, 12.2, 13.2

Genealogy, 13.13
Genetic manipulation, 21.7
Geology, 19.18, 19.21
Germany, 24.6
Ghosts, 10.38, 17.4, 17.7, 17.20, 23.10, 23.11, 23.15–17, 23.19
Gliding, 22.3
Grandparents, 5.8, 6.4, 6.6, 6.15, 6.35–38, 7.3, 10.24, 10.34, 10.48, 17.29
Great Britain, 3.23, 24.9

Hawaii, 10.48
Hispanics, 13.2
Holidays, 15.1, 23.17
Holocaust, 5.7, 5.10, 13.3
Homeless persons, 21.9
Homesteading, 1.14
Homosexuality, 6.25, 6.36, 10.29, 21.3, 21.10
Honor, personal, 22.8
Horror stories, 7.22, 21.7
Horses, 2.2, 2.5, 2.7, 2.9, 2.12, 9.7, 10.22, 10.29
Human body, 11.6, 19.13

Illinois, 24.12
Immigrants, 5.6
Independence, 21.21
Inventors, 3.7, 3.24
Israel, 24.11

Jealousy, 6.33, 10.25
Jews, 5.1, 5.6, 5.7, 5.10, 13.3

Kidnapping, 1.4, 1.6, 1.10, 17.6, 17.8, 17.9, 17.11, 17.13, 17.22, 20.9

Labor strikes, 21.4
Latin America, 3.22, 21.1
Learning disabilities, 21.22
Legends, 8.3, 8.4
Lifestyle changes, 6.9, 6.23, 10.44, 10.53, 16.15
Love, 4.1, 4.5, 10.3, 10.4, 16.1–15, 17.34, 21.8

Magic and magicians, 7.7, 7.8, 7.20, 7.24, 17.24, 23.2, 23.3, 23.13
Marriage, 12.7
Massachusetts, 6.39
Mental health services, 11.3
Mental illness, 6.14, 6.20, 6.21, 11.2
Mexican Americans, 3.15
Mexico, 1.3, 6.19, 10.20, 10.40
Mice, 7.9
Microscopes, 19.2
Migrant workers, 9.1, 21.15
Military leaders, 3.32
Millionaires, 3.6, 3.16
Minnesota, 6.30
Missing persons, 6.32
Moneymaking projects, 6.9, 9.1, 10.23, 10.44, 15.4, 16.15, 21.2
Morocco, 17.29
Mothers and daughters, 6.12, 6.22, 7.3, 7.15, 10.48
Mothers and sons, 6.34, 20.7
Motorcycles, 15.7
Mountain life, 1.14, 17.5
Movies, 10.27
Murder, 6.20, 17.10, 17.17, 17.18, 17.23, 17.34, 17.35
Music and musicians, 6.39, 10.30, 10.32, 10.43, 10.47, 10.49, 13.9, 17.30, 19.1, 21.2
Mystery and detective stories, 5.11, 7.21, 17.1–41, 21.18, 23.6, 23.10

Native Americans, 3.5, 3.9, 3.10, 3.13, 3.21, 3.26, 3.27, 5.5, 5.8, 5.12, 5.13
Nature, 1.9, 2.1, 2.3, 4.2, 24.2, 24.8, 24.14
New York, 24.5
New Zealand, 24.1
Nuclear protests, 21.19, 22.10

Old age, 6.3, 6.15, 6.35, 9.4, 9.6, 10.24, 10.31

Old West, The, 1.5
Organ transplants, 19.13
Orphans, 6.33, 12.3
Outdoor recreation, 24.2, 24.8, 24.14
Outer space, 19.3, 19.15, 20.13

Paleontology, 5.5, 12.2
Perseverance, 10.38
Physical disabilities, 2.4, 6.27, 7.11, 9.8, 17.19, 17.22, 22.4
Physics, 19.5
Pirates, 1.7
Plague, The, 21.19
Poetry, 18.1–8
Police, 1.6
Political beliefs, 6.7
Political prisoners, 21.1
Politics and political leaders, 3.11, 3.14, 3.15, 3.30, 13.7, 13.8, 13.11, 13.15, 20.12
Popularity, 10.10, 10.18, 10.46, 10.50, 15.6
Pottery, 14.3
Pranks, 10.12, 22.12
Prejudice, 3.25, 5.1, 5.4, 5.9, 6.11, 21.3
Presidents, U.S., 3.14, 13.8, 13.15
Psychic powers, 20.5, 20.8, 23.19

Quests, 1.15

Rabbits, 8.2
Race relations, 3.25, 5.4, 5.9, 21.8
Rape, 21.3
Rats, 7.12
Rebellion, 10.19
Religion, 6.22
Revenge, 10.35, 17.39, 23.16
Revolutionaries, 3.22
Robots, 17.2
Royalty, 3.23
Runaways, 6.8, 10.2, 10.12, 12.6, 17.28
Running, 10.45, 23.18

Satire, 15.8, 15.11
School, 10.4, 10.13, 10.28, 10.35, 10.36, 10.50, 10.53, 15.3, 15.6, 16.12, 17.37, 17.39, 18.3, 21.11, 21.22, 22.6, 22.12
Science fiction, 20.1–13
Scientists, 3.18
Sea lions, 2.10
Self-discovery, 1.9, 5.12, 6.28, 10.13, 16.8, 17.28
Self-image, 5.2, 10.27, 10.43, 10.50, 16.1, 21.22, 22.5
Self-reliance, 10.33
Sex education, 10.17

Sex roles, 6.13, 6.17, 22.6
Sexual abuse, 21.12, 21.20
Short stories, 7.22, 8.1, 8.2, 8.4, 23.1
Skiing, 17.16
Slavery, 3.17
Small-town life, 10.8, 10.10, 10.22, 10.41, 15.5
Soccer, 10.28
South Africa, 3.25, 5.4, 5.9
Southwest, U.S., 13.2
Spain, history, 13.10
Speechmaking, 14.5
Sports, 3.28, 3.29, 18.5, 19.11, 22.1–13
Sports, history, 3.29
Sports records, 22.2
Sports science, 19.11
Stepparents, 6.1, 10.11
Storytelling, 6.30
Suicide, 4.4, 17.3, 21.5, 21.13, 21.20
Supernatural, 7.22, 17.14, 23.1–20
Survival, 1.8, 1.11, 1.12, 10.2, 20.2
Suspense, 17.4, 17.31
Swamps, 17.41

Teachers, 21.15
Telescopes, 19.4
Tennessee, 24.4
Theater, 6.4, 10.16, 10.26, 17.7, 17.36
Time travel, 1.13, 7.4, 20.3, 20.10, 23.14
Trivia, 13.4, 13.14, 15.9, 22.2

Uncles, 10.29, 15.7
United States, history, 3.5, 3.9–11, 3.14, 3.21, 3.26, 3.27, 3.32, 13.4, 13.6–8, 13.10, 13.12
United States, politics and government, 3.11, 13.7, 13.11

Vacations, 9.11, 15.10
Vietnam War, 6.21, 9.10, 10.5, 10.15, 10.40, 18.7

Washington, D.C., 24.13
Weight problems, 9.9, 10.6
Whales, 19.16
White House, The, 13.8, 13.15
Wildlife conservation, 2.7, 2.8, 2.10, 6.19, 19.16
Wishes, 23.3, 23.7
Witchcraft, 7.5, 23.5, 23.6, 23.9, 23.18
World War II, 5.7, 5.10, 6.17, 12.3, 12.4
Wrestling, 22.8
Writers and writing, 10.8, 10.22, 14.1

Zoology, 2.11

Editor

William G. McBride is professor of English at Colorado State University and executive secretary-treasurer of the Colorado Language Arts Society, Colorado's professional organization of language arts teachers. He has taught at all levels and in rural and suburban environments. In addition to articles and book reviews, he coauthored (with Ruth Cline) the book *A Guide to Literature for Young Adults: Background, Selection, and Use.* He has served on the board of directors for ALAN and for SIGNAL and now serves on the local board of education and on NCTE's Secondary Section Committee.

U. S. GRANT MIDDLE SCHOOL